What People Are Saying About
Serving Time, Serving Others

"*Serving Time, Serving Others* demonstrates the positive affects helping others has on relationships and one's self-esteem. These stories illustrate the resiliency and compassion of the human spirit. An inspiration to corrections staff and inmates alike."

Maria Panicali, Psy.D.
Clinical Psychologist

"This book is like a mirror that reflects the light and warmth of unselfish love and caring that is given so freely by those that are doing good behind bars."

Edward Anthony Smith
Inmate

"The stories in *Serving Time, Serving Others* reveal the impact faith, hope and love have had on the lives of those served as well as those who serve."

Gene Bal
Kairos prison volunteer

"Great stories about real people who find a way to be kind in the most difficult of circumstances. This is a book that reminds us to be optimistic."

Dr. Jeffrey Ian Ross and
Dr. Stephen C. Richards
Authors, *Behind Bars: Surviving Prison*
and *Convict Criminology*

"These stories reveal the light which shines brightly in a world most people paint as dim and heartless. Everyone should read this book and see that the human heart beats with love everywhere, even in prison."

Marcia Reynolds, M.A., M.Ed.
Ex-inmate, professional speaker
and author, *Outsmart Your Brain!*

"Teenagers, as well as adults, will be inspired to reach out to others after reading these stories, because *Serving Time, Serving Others* illustrates that no heart is too small and no effort too big to make difference."

Catholic Chaplain

"We hear so many stories about prison that scare us to death. This book helps to lift that 'black cloud.' When I read all the wonderful things that have happened behind bars, it gives me hope."

Scott Heap
Inmate

"The stories in *Serving Time, Serving Others* are beautiful, living experiences of real people in difficult circumstances, sharing their love and caring nature for others in a godly way."

Fr. Gabriel Calvo
Founder of Marriage Encounter

"*Serving Time, Serving Others* contains positive attributes that spiritual people strive for: forgiveness, hope, self-esteem, giving and purpose. These real life stories, born of difficult circumstances, demonstrate that the world can change—one heart at a time."

Gordon Green
Chaplain, New Brunswick, Canada

"Men, women and youth who are separated from our society are capable of performing acts of kindness. *Serving Time, Serving Others* illustrates positive and enlightening examples."

Clark Bartram
Professional fitness model,
personal trainer and prison volunteer

"The powerful stories in *Serving Time, Serving Others* show that hope is very much alive in our penal institutions."

Don Nunes
Supervisor, Public Library Outreach Services

"*Serving Time, Serving Others* encourages everyone to make a positive difference; whether they work, reside, minister, visit or volunteer behind bars."

Marion S. Reynolds, Jr.
Coordinator of Chaplaincy/Institutional Ministries

"These poignant stories open the eyes and soften the heart, providing insight into acts of kindness behind the walls."

Brian Brookheart
Author, *A Prisoner: Released*
Ex-inmate, Successful Business Owner

Serving Time, Serving Others

*Acts of Kindness by Inmates,
Prison Staff,
Victims, and Volunteers*

Tom Lagana
Laura Lagana

SERVING TIME, SERVING OTHERS:
Acts of Kindness by Inmates, Prison Staff, Victims, and Volunteers
Copyright ©2003 Tom Lagana and Laura Lagana
All rights reserved.

Published by Fruit-Bearer Publishing
A Branch of Candy's Creations
P.O. Box 777, Georgetown, DE 19947
(302) 856-6649 • Fax (302) 856-7742
fruitbearer.publishing@verizon.net
www.fruitbearer.com
Graphic design by Candy Abbott with Suzette Stewart
Cover design by Suzette Stewart
Printed in the USA

Library of Congress Control Number: 2003113222
Self Help • Inspiration • Prison

ISBN 1-886068-06-2

Other books by Laura Lagana and Tom Lagana:
Chicken Soup for the Prisoner's Soul
Chicken Soup for the Volunteer's Soul
Touched by Angels of Mercy

To Order This Book

Send check or money order for $14.95 plus $3.05 for shipping and handling ($18 total) for each copy of Serving Time, Serving Others. Cost based on Media Mail shipping in the continental U.S. Allow 2 weeks for delivery after payment received. Check or money order payable to "Success Solutions."

Serving Time, Serving Others – Purchase
P.O. Box 7816
Wilmington, DE 19803

(Special quantity discounts available.)
E-mail: Tom@TomLagana.com
www.TomLagana.com

Dedication

With gratitude, love and respect, we dedicate this book to God, prisoners, former inmates, family and friends of those incarcerated, prison personnel, volunteers, victims of crime and their loved ones, and all who make a positive difference behind the razor wire.

In memory of contributing authors whom we grew to know and love:

Bob Kennington
Rex Moore, Jr.
Steven Dodrill
Lou Torok

THE IN SIDE
by Matt Matteo

Reprinted by permission of Matt Matteo.

Table of Contents

"As an inmate, the best thing you can do for your incarcerated friends is to never want to see them again. I don't mean to stop loving them. Instead, choose to be the one to show them that you can change your life. Get out, set goals, then move toward meeting your goals step by step until you find yourself living what you dared to dream while in jail. Your success is the best gift you can give your friends. And if your paths cross again outside, you can celebrate together."

—Marcia Reynolds, M.A., M.Ed.
Former inmate and current successful business owner

"Peace cannot be kept by force. It can only be achieved by understanding."

—Albert Einstein

Foreword

Burl Cain, CCE
Warden of Louisiana State Penitentiary

I am humbled to be given an opportunity to be a part of this book. Prisons are places in which real changes can occur, primarily because they are places void of most worldly distractions. They are full of opportunities for meaningful self-analysis. More and more we see that the persons destined to live out the rest of their days behind bars have great ability to learn and even discover hidden talents when given the opportunity to be creative.

It's all about corrections—not punishment. It's simple. We pay attention, we set good examples, and we reward positive behavior. We teach compassion, and we respect life and especially people's feelings. We can say hello and tell jokes without fear of our authority, careers and, most of all, security being compromised.

It's all about choices. Freedom always is. The saying, "Life is hard," is very true. Life is also what you make it. Prison makes us reflect on who we are—it makes us want to be better—it makes us cope with what we have done. Prison makes us question our very existence.

The stories in this book are written by real men and women who have learned hard life-lessons. Their willingness to let you into "their prisons" is commendable. It is the essence of what ties us all together: being human, sharing our stories with those like us in order to ultimately touch the mind, heart and soul. This book is proof that there is hope—hope for us all to learn to live together in peace.

The Prayer

Roy Anthony Borges

*M*ay the peace, love, joy and happiness of life be with us today. May all our suspicious doubts and fears be erased so that Your light may shine forth in us all.

Give us the strength to stop blaming other people for our problems and the wisdom to check ourselves out first, for then we will discover that a majority of our problems, suspicions and wrong deeds are our own fault.

Lord, teach us to remember that we pay a price for the lessons that we learn in this life and that no matter how smart or tough we think we are, we can be had. The race of life is not won by the swift and the greedy. Let me be able to be the same whether I have abundance or poverty.

No one owes us anything, and no one in our life is going to be totally true and faithful to us. So let us stop looking for it and recognize that no one is perfect, that people are human and make mistakes. Add forgiveness to our ways and rid us of all bitterness.

Replace in our hearts a desire to know You, for we know the rewards shall be great.

May we always be grateful for being alive and realize that no matter what the problems or circumstances may be You will carry us through them.

Life is too short to waste time on the things we can't change. Let us think positively about today, for tomorrow is not guaranteed to anyone. Amen.

Acknowledgments

S*erving Time, Serving Others* has been a fast-paced, compelling, and gratifying project. We are grateful for everyone who assisted us, especially the following individuals:

Our sons, Brandon and Daniel, and their families who have blessed us with their abiding love and support, each and every day.

Jacqueline, our daughter-in-law, who so generously reviewed every story, offering valuable input and suggestions.

Mom, Catherine Jennie Gilardi Lagana, who provides steadfast insight and encouragement, urging us to continue living our passion.

Linda and Bob, our sister and brother-in-law, who eagerly lend an open ear and heart, at the precise times we need it most.

Candy Abbott, who placed her own writing projects on the side-burner while polishing and formatting our manuscript to prepare it for printing.

Jane Hudson, our proofreader, and Suzette Stewart, our graphic artist.

Jean Hull Herman, friend and accomplished poet who shared her expertise by editing and offering feedback on the poems.

Linda Bekiarian, valued friend, who is always willing to help out, without question.

Danny Casalenuovo and Adam Perry, whose letters touched our hearts, helping us to see that, without a doubt, we needed to create another prison-related book.

We are grateful for each person who took the time to submit stories, poems and other fruits of their labor for consideration. While many were outstanding, they sometimes were not a compatible fit for the overall configuration of our book.

We appreciate all who helped make this book possible, in particular our contributing authors and cartoonists.

From the Far Side of the Wall

Chaplain Rod Carter
Ex-offender

1. God helps those who help themselves.
2. There but for the grace of God go I.
3. Whatever you are trying to avoid won't go away until you confront it.
4. A law of divine reciprocity says that we reap what we sow.
5. Freedom is knowing how to remember the weight of your chains after they've been removed.
6. How we treat others is how we treat God.
7. Prisons are monuments to neglected youth.
8. Because crime comes from the community, the solution must come from the community.
9. Criminal behavior is, for the most part, learned behavior.
10. Society has only two kinds of offenders—those who get caught, and the rest of us.
11. You don't need a map of the Promised Land before leaving Egypt.

"Everybody can be great . . . because anybody can serve. You don't have to have a college degree to serve. You don't have to make your subject and verb agree to serve. You only need a heart full of grace. A soul generated by love."

—*Martin Luther King, Jr.*

Introduction

Why would a professional engineer and a registered nurse co-author a book about the good things that happen in prison?

More than ten years ago, inspired by two inmates, one in Oklahoma and another in Delaware, we were summoned to begin volunteering in prison. We came to the realization that we all have stories—including inmates. We have seen and heard about personal accounts of the transforming power of kindness and compassion that, every now and then, becomes a channel to forgiveness, change, and freedom.

Today, with more than two million men, women, and children behind bars in the United States, correctional facilities continue to proliferate and the vicious cycle of crime, imprisonment, and recidivism seems unstoppable. Although the countless factors that contribute to this dilemma are not the focus in this text, they do affect everyone.

We all journey through life together, struggling to discover a meaningful purpose to our existence. During this journey, we all make choices, decisions, and mistakes. No one is perfect. Most of us receive help along the way, when we need it most. And, once in a while, we have the rewarding opportunity to repay the favor by giving someone else a helping hand.

Society can benefit and learn from these personal accounts of benevolence. Stories from the inside can illuminate the darkest of places, providing inspiration, insight and, we hope, a call to action. You are invited to read and reflect on these stories through the eyes of the authors and to be inspired to help make our world a better place.

A view from inside the barbed wire sheds light on the need for treatment, continued education and the learning of a trade by the inmates. Helping inmates become productive members of our society requires joint effort—everyone working together to create successful solutions.

Our objectives for writing and compiling stories for this book are threefold. First and foremost, we want to give inmates hope: to empower prisoners to do as much good as they can in their current environment by providing constructive examples of what others have accomplished under similar circumstances.

Our second objective is to encourage prison administrators and staff to allow more programs to be brought into correctional facilities. We can all work together as a team to facilitate the rehabilitation of inmates and build their self-esteem, thereby increasing the likelihood that they will succeed—both inside the prison walls, as well as on the outside upon their release.

Our last objective is to express appreciation and gratitude to everyone who volunteers behind bars and to encourage others to follow in their footsteps so that they, too, can reap rich emotional and spiritual rewards.

Inmates, prison staff members, loved-ones of those who are incarcerated, victims, and volunteers can all make a significant difference and have a positive impact toward a more peaceful world.

So, why would a professional engineer and a registered nurse co-author a book about the good things that happen in prison? The only logical answer is far from logical—it radiates from the heart and soul. We answered the call, and we continue to respond.

Yes, we all have a story to tell. The challenge is to listen—and to take positive action.

"Power is the faculty or capacity to act, the strength and potency to accomplish something. It is the vital energy to make choices and decisions. It also includes the capacity to overcome deeply embedded habits and to cultivate higher, more effective ones."

—Stephen R. Covey

1

Discovering a Meaningful Purpose

"Each of our acts makes a statement as to our purpose."

—*Leo Buscaglia*

Serving Moral Time

Gary K. Farlow

*P*art of the Jaycee creed reads that "Service to humanity is the best work of life." Today's rising crime rates and an ever-growing prison population make it easy to overlook the many inmates who put forth the effort to "give back" to the community.

Earthquakes are fairly common in California, but typically only the major tremors make the news. The quake that rocked San Francisco in the early 1990s occurred while I was at the Caledonia Prison Farm in the coastal plane of North Carolina. At the time, and unlike many other prisons in the state, Caledonia did not have an "Inmate Service Club" such as a Jaycees chapter. But it did have two inmates named "Big Sam" and "L.A."

Obviously, L.A. was a native of Los Angeles, who had grown up in the streets of the East Side Barrios in the City of Angels. Big Sam's name suited him well. At more than 250 pounds, Sam was a former jeweler from St. Louis whose love for gold must have had something to do with the "golden heart" he possessed toward his fellow man.

"Hey, L.A., wake up, Man," I heard Sam say early one morning. "A big quake rocked San Francisco last night, and the city's a mess."

L.A. bolted out of bed and sat mesmerized by the scenes of utter devastation playing across the TV screen. As the horror of what a major earthquake can bring sank into the minds of the inmates gathered around the TV, the minds of L.A. and Big Sam were already focusing on the aftermath.

"Hey, Man! What's up?" came the cries of protest as L.A. stepped up and flipped the TV off. He calmly raised his hands. Amazingly, the protests ebbed to hear what he had to say.

"Look, Guys, most of you know I'm from Los Angeles. I don't know how many of you have ever lived through an earthquake, so let me tell you. There's no fear like it. Those people out there have lost everything. They're gonna need some help."

"Help?" said one young inmate. "Hey, Dude, that's what the government's for."

"Yeah," spoke up another. "They got the Red Cross and stuff that'll help 'em out."

"Right," still another said. "And we're just a bunch of convicts. What can we do anyway?"

Not discouraged, L.A. listened to what everyone had to say; then he spoke. "Fellas, I'll grant that we're all prisoners who society feels have little to contribute, but this is an opportunity for us not only to prove such a belief wrong but also to give something of ourselves. To serve some 'moral time,'" L.A. stated.

"Moral time?" asked one of the gathered inmates. "What're you talking about, L.A.?"

"What I'm talking about is doing something for someone else. Not because we have to but because we want to. Doing the right thing. Helping another person in need."

"Just how do you plan for us to go about it?" asked Big Sam, his interest clearly reflected in the faces of about 30 fellow inmates who had been listening to the exchange.

"Well," began L.A., "none of us has a lot of money."

This statement was quickly met with nods and groans of agreement. The typical inmate in North Carolina earns an "incentive wage" of either 40 or 70 cents a day.

"But," L.A. continued, "we can raise some money."

L.A. and Big Sam put together a fundraising campaign that included the sale of donuts, pizzas, and even a car wash where prison staff could get their automobiles washed and waxed. The entire prison, inmates and staff, were quickly galvanized into unity with the goal of raising money to provide some relief to the victims of San Francisco's recent quake.

In just two months, a little more than $2,000 was raised and sent to the San Francisco Earthquake Relief Fund. A sense of positive accomplishment prevailed over the prison for quite some time. The event was a first for many prisoners who learned the pleasure of giving selflessly to others and the joy and peace it brings. Random acts of kindness replaced acts of violence as prisoners shared a common goal, working with prison staff to help the suffering thousands of miles away.

On the day that the check was placed in the mail, the warden had the kitchen serve a special breakfast to celebrate the achievement. As inmates sat down with staff to share donuts, ham biscuits, and fresh fruit, everyone was reminded of the brotherhood of mankind. Such a brotherhood supersedes the superficial divisions of man from man, inmate from free citizen, one status from another status. We all learned that "Service to humanity is the best work of life."

[EDITOR'S NOTE: For more information on the Jaycees, contact P.O. Box 7, Tulsa, OK 74102-0007; Web site: http://www.usjaycees.org.]

A Life that Matters

Douglas Burgess

*T*he officer tugged impatiently at my shackled wrists, but I paused on the courthouse steps anyway to take a last look at my hometown—a place I would never again see after the judge's sentence of "life" in prison for my part in conspiring to commit murder. A second tug, this one more insistent, quickly reminded me that my life was no longer my own and that it was essentially over.

After a few months' existence in a dank, dimly-lit prison cell, surrounded by insects and an unceasing cycle of violence, I was pretty much convinced that my life was both hopeless and worthless. I asked myself time and again, *How can I do something good to make amends for my crime when everything at the Reformatory* (ominously nicknamed "Gladiator School") *is negative, selfish and hateful?* The answer came when I enrolled in the prison's college extension program.

Professor Gochberg taught humanities, which dealt in part with the Holocaust. Through his tireless and personable explanations, he taught me that hope always exists, regardless of the conditions that surround people. How they choose to respond separates them from animals. From that moment on, I chose to find some way to make my life meaningful and useful to others, no matter how small the contribution.

Later, after learning how to develop and run charitable projects through the Jaycees, I searched for ways to best use my new skills. I organized food and clothing drives for the needy, found ways to purchase toys for destitute children, and assembled teams of talented prisoner-artists to make "get well" cards for the elderly and children in local hospitals. The best project I was ever involved in was a series of anti-crime videos designed for school children.

The first video, appropriately titled *Do Your Own Time*, featured Ross, an energetic Canadian volunteer, interviewing five other prisoners and me. In our efforts to keep youth from breaking the law, we considered no topic in our program taboo. We discussed what brought us to prison, told what our daily lives were like, and offered advice on how to stay out of prison to our young viewers.

Do Your Own Time became an overnight success. Ross received requests for his video presentation from all over Canada and the United States. With so many demands placed on his time, Ross wasn't able to visit us for several months. When he did arrive, he came with an armful of letters from school children and teachers expressing their thanks, commenting on our messages and even offering advice on how to improve our video.

One letter stood out from the rest because of its shocking admission. In a very matter-of-fact tone, a young student explained how she'd come to the conclusion that her life wasn't what she wanted it to be. She wanted to be popular, and she hated the fact that she wasn't. She felt no one understood her, so she intended to commit suicide after school that day. Her plan was chilling in its simplicity. She would go home, overdose on prescription drugs and be found hours later, lying dead in the privacy of her bed. But that was the day Ross presented our video at her school.

In her letter she wrote, "Watching your video made me realize that life is what I choose to make it, and it's too precious to cut short." She concluded, "Thanks to each of you for helping me understand that my life really does matter—even if I'm not the most popular girl in school."

The joy I experienced at reading this young woman's letter was indescribable. After taking a life, being partly responsible for saving one remains one of the greatest accomplishments I have experienced. This girl's choice to live, and to lead a productive life confirmed the fact that I can still do something to benefit others. Like her, I realized that my life matters.

Salvaging the lives of the hopeless costs very little yet gives so much in return. This was Professor Gochberg's greatest lesson, and one he would be proud to know is still being taught.

[EDITOR'S NOTE: For more information on the Jaycees, contact P.O. Box 7, Tulsa, OK 74102-0007; Web site: http://www.usjaycees.org.]

"No man is so poor as to have nothing worth giving. Give what you have. To someone it may be better than you dare to think."

—Henry Wadsworth Longfellow

Reading History

Pooja Krishna

As he dragged his feet toward school, Joshua wanted to kick something or smash a few windows. He was already ten minutes late. *Just my luck,* he thought. He knew trying to pinch the penknife from the store was dumb—and dumber, still, to get caught. But the punishment was the worst part. They didn't lock him up in prison, and even Pop's thrashing would have been okay, even though it hurt really bad. *Anything would be better than sitting in a crazy classroom, reading stuff aloud to a blind man.*

The judge had sentenced him to the Sheriff's Community Program for Juveniles. "Juvenile!" he spat. In another six months he would turn fifteen. He was hardly a kid, but had anyone listened? Instead, they had told him he would have to work off his punishment by working twice a week, all summer. *Just how did these people figure out this smart guy stuff? It's darned simple—they have an attitude problem, and they're taking it out on me.*

He stomped into the school to the assigned room, where a man waited. *Geez! He's ancient. Older than Pop, even.* Except for the dark glasses, you would never know that the man couldn't see. Especially when he unerringly offered his hand in Josh's direction.

"Mr. Joshua Kinley, right?" he asked. "I'm Professor Harlan Peritt. Thanks for coming to help me out."

At least someone around here is grateful that I'm wasting my summer. "It's okay," Josh muttered ungraciously, "They didn't give me a choice."

The old man didn't respond to the obvious attack. "Shall we get down to it, then?" he asked, handing over a fat, heavy volume. The professor continued, despite Josh's groans. "This story is based on the war between the British and Napoleon's France. It isn't available in Braille or in audio, hence this session."

Josh glared at him, opening the book anyway. *I'll be bored out of my mind reading history, of all things. But what else can I expect from this old fogey?* Josh began reading very rapidly, in a stilted manner. Harlan Peritt didn't say anything. He just listened quietly.

By the time Josh reached page fifteen, something happened. He started to get interested in the tale of the eighteen-year-old British soldier, wounded and alone in a French village. Through the next few pages, Josh felt the soldier's anger, bitterness, fear . . . and loneliness. *It's almost like they've written about . . . me.*

"Thank you, Joshua," the Professor remarked, two hours later. "We'll meet again on Friday."

Friday came; and, while Joshua still wasn't thrilled about his volunteer service, it didn't seem so terrible. Besides, he was curious about the soldier. This time he read more slowly, paid more attention. At the end of the session, Harlan said warmly, "You have a good voice. I enjoyed that." Josh didn't take the compliment seriously; he just mumbled a response and left.

The following week, after yet another meeting, Harlan remarked, "I sense a lot of anger inside you, Joshua."

"What would you know?" Josh retorted bitterly, "You can't even see."

"True. But it sometimes helps to talk about what's bothering you," Harlan said gently. "Think about it."

The summer progressed, as did Joshua. He hardly noticed when he stayed well beyond his two-hour reading session. Without realizing it, he began telling Harlan things that he'd never mentioned to anyone else—like his Pop's drinking, the contempt of his neighbors and his isolation at school.

For the most part, Harlan listened, with only an occasional comment. Josh was no longer desperately waiting for summer's end. *The Professor may be old, but he's not dumb. Besides, no one has cared to listen to me ever since Mom died.*

When Josh asked him about his family, Harlan shook his head and said, "I have no one. My wife is gone, and we didn't have any children," he added sadly.

Finally, Josh's punishment ended. After their final sitting was over, Harlan shook hands with him. "I'm happy to have made a new friend, Joshua. I know your allotted time is over, but would you like to read for me at my home after school?"

Harlan's okay, but it wouldn't do to sound too eager. Josh pretended to think it over and finally agreed. He went several times a week to Harlan's home. He read aloud, whatever book or passage the old man wanted. The stories were sometimes great but often dull. But Josh didn't mind. He located passages from textbooks, wrote material that Harlan dictated, met some studious types who didn't look down at him, and explored the hidden treasures of Harlan's library. *Not all those history books are so bad.*

Josh was surprised that he enjoyed reading some of the books, especially when Harlan gave him the edition about the soldier.

"But I never asked for it," he protested.

"Keep it. It's a gift," came the simple reply.

One evening, several months later, Harlan mentioned that he was leaving town. Josh tried to sound nonchalant, but it was a poor effort. He soon realized, much to his immense relief, that Harlan wasn't going away for good.

"You'll definitely come back?" Josh asked skeptically.

"I promised, didn't I? I am going to Princeton for only one term. I'll be back by spring. Meanwhile, you have to honor your promise of keeping up with your schoolwork and not picking a fight with anyone."

"Okay," Josh agreed. "Say, Harlan," he asked casually, "When you come back, do you need any more help with your book? Research, I mean. I could read you stuff and make notes for you." He placed an earnest hand on Harlan's arm. "And you don't even have to give me anything."

The professor said nothing. He only smiled at Joshua and nodded. The evening before he left, Harlan Peritt had a visitor.

"I understand you're leaving tomorrow," said Sheriff Dylan, "I wanted to thank you for everything."

"There's no need," came the calm reply.

"Oh, but there is," the Sheriff repudiated. "You volunteered as an advisor for our community program and gave valuable input, for Josh Kinley in particular. He is one reformed boy. It's no secret most people here thought he was heading down the same road as his old man."

"Joshua is a very fine young man. He was hurting too much."

"Sure, but no one else wanted to touch him until you agreed to help out."

Harlan was silent for a moment. "You know Sheriff, these last few months with Joshua filled a great vacuum in my life—one I didn't even know existed. So please don't thank me," he added in a voice heavy with rare emotion, "because with Joshua, I don't know who helped whom."

"History is the version of past events that people have decided to agree upon."

—*Napoleon*

A Life-Long Enterprise

Diane Hamill Metzger

As a fifty-four-year-old prisoner of twenty-eight years' duration, serving a life sentence, I have been acquainted with hundreds of volunteers from various organizations and of varied persuasions. Assuming that my role was to be a recipient of the many benefits provided by the army of volunteers who daily visited my place of incarceration, I was surprised to learn that my greatest satisfaction would take place when I became a volunteer.

My first role as a volunteer began after I completed the course as a Laubach Literacy Volunteer. I approached the whole endeavor with more than a little hesitancy, because I felt that I would never have the patience to work with adults who couldn't read. I liked fast learners, college students, gifted children, and those who could catch on the first time I showed them how to do something. The thought of patiently reiterating the same instructions and lessons to new learners, over and over again, did not appeal to me.

Then I met Susan. She was serving a life sentence just like me, except that she had come to prison at the undeveloped age of fourteen. Susan couldn't read or write. Her background had been a turbulent and tragic one, and it didn't include school.

Her only living relatives were her brother and her dad, both of whom were also incarcerated. Her main goal was to be able to write them letters, and to be able to read any letters they might write back to her. I knew that teaching Susan would be an arduous task because she didn't trust people and didn't like sitting still for more than five minutes at a time. Most significantly, Susan didn't believe that she could learn or that she had any self-worth whatsoever. Changing that negative self-image was going to be even more difficult than learning words and constructing sentences.

What a challenge! Days turned into weeks—weeks into months. Finally the day came when Susan asked me, "Do you think I can write good enough to send my dad a letter?" Without a word, I slid her a blank piece of paper and handed her a pen.

As I sat there and watched, she painstakingly printed, "Dear Dad. How are you? I am fine. I love you. Please write me back. Love, Susan." She looked up at me and our eyes met. Both of us were crying. As Susan hugged me and headed off for her housing unit with the precious letter clutched in her hand, I knew then not only why people become volunteers but why some of them make it a life-long enterprise.

[EDITOR'S NOTE: For information on Laubach Literacy, contact 1320 Jamesville Av, Syracuse, NY 13210; Web site: http://www.laubach.org.]

"Happiness is not a destination. It is a way of life."
—*Burton Hills*

Just Say Yes

Dan Millstein

Around 1990, I was introduced to an attorney for a local ACLU (American Civil Liberties Union). In the middle of our conversation, she asked me, "Where did you go to school, Dan?"

My ego said, *Tell her Harvard . . . she'll never know.* But I told the truth. "I was a street kid. I never even went to high school," I replied. That answer changed my life.

She told me about a young man being held in the local youth prison facility. Even though his arrest and charges were out of proportion to his crime, he trusted no one. Facing a prison sentence because he wouldn't accept help from anyone, he even considered the ACLU to be "the enemy." This boy, who had a long record of "calling for help," was now looking at nine years in prison for stealing a pizza from a delivery truck parked near his house.

"Would you go to the prison with me, Dan, and just talk to this boy?" asked the attorney.

As a last resort, she thought that I might be able to help. The life of this young man sounded a lot like mine when I was his age. Not knowing what to expect, I answered, "Sure."

Later that week, I met Matt in the visiting room. We sat at a plastic table on round steel seats secured to the table's frame. Matt, an immense, muscular teenager with heavily tattooed arms, appeared to be much older than sixteen. *No wonder they wanted to put him away,* I thought.

He had a distinct intensity about him—I felt it even before he spoke. Extending my hand, I introduced myself. "Hello Matt, I'm Dan. I must confess . . . I don't know exactly why I'm here. But I'm willing to tell you my own story . . . if you're willing to listen." Matt nodded in agreement.

As I shared my own painful childhood with him, I caught a glimpse of a tear or two sliding down his cheeks, perhaps in a sympathetic response to mine. I hadn't let myself become this vulnerable before. *But why not?* I thought. *I'll probably never see this kid again anyway.*

Before long, I was pleading with him. "Don't wait another moment. Don't hold it inside like I did. I know you, Matt. You are me." We both cried. In that fate-filled moment and in the many visits I had with Matt after our first encounter, Visions for Prisons was born. My destiny was sealed and my life's purpose fulfilled.

Ten years later, Matt popped back into my life. He had become a father, and he held a steady job. I'm glad I had the chance to thank him.

[EDITOR'S NOTE: For information on Visions for Prisons, contact P.O. Box 1631, Costa Mesa, CA 92628; http://www.visionsforprisons.org.]

"Inside you there's an artist you don't know about . . . Say yes quickly, if you know you've known it from before the beginning of the universe."
—*Jalai ud-Din Rumi*

A Ten-Cent Pen

Matt Matteo

All rise!" Everyone stood as the judge glided into the courtroom, black robe flowing behind with each long stride. He sat down and began arranging his papers. The assistant district attorney, confident and smiling, spoke to a suited colleague and opened his black leather briefcase. From within, he produced a heavy file with my name scrawled on it in bold letters. Then it struck me. *This hearing could rewrite the rest of my life.*

I had little cause for optimism. After all, the judge wasn't obligated to alter my sentence, and regrettably my crimes were violent. I thought about what I had going for me. Nine years free of any trouble—no small feat in prison—only two misconducts, both for minor "write ups," which resulted in warnings.

Initially, I was assigned to a medium-security prison and later transferred to a minimum-security facility. I was headed in the right direction, but the philosophy in the Department of Corrections was to first treat those inmates who were close to release. As a result, years away from eligibility, I'd received no rehabilitation or programming in more than nine years of prison time. My lawyer had almost nothing to work with.

Altering my sentence had to come from evidence of a positive change, so I photocopied a collection of my published paintings, illustrations, and awards that I had won in recent years. I submitted them to my lawyer with the hope and a prayer that they would prove I'd reformed.

After my name and case number were announced, my lawyer got up and strode to the podium. Ankles shackled, I shuffled to meet him. Introductions were made and the judge explained the purpose of the hearing. No one asked me a thing as the prosecutor established the legitimacy of my lengthy sentence and referred to a wealth of documents. My lawyer countered those claims while the judge rocked in his chair. Having no role in the hearing, I felt as if I were listening to someone else's fate being decided.

Interrupting the illusion, my lawyer turned and asked if I'd tell the court of the successes and awards I'd earned while in prison. Disoriented by the request that I speak on my own behalf, for the first time, I whispered to my lawyer, "How is my art relevant?"

His answer—a blank stare. I gathered he didn't know either. I had no organized or carefully planned speech, but my words just came out. While I spoke, I exhausted every memory of my paintings that appeared in journals, of my cartoons published in several states, of the calendars and greeting cards, the murals, tutoring . . . and on and on I went, hoping this would reflect more on who I was than the thick file.

When I couldn't think of anything else, I stood in silence, waiting for the unknown. The judge, apparently considering what I'd said, shuffled through his papers and paused to gaze out the window for a moment. Then he turned to me and inquired, "And how is this relevant, Mr. Matteo?" I was speechless. This was the very question I'd asked my lawyer only minutes before. Unable to provide an answer, I felt my hopes sink.

That question has echoed in my mind ever since. From the carpeted courtroom to the cold county jail, to the sheriff's cruiser and back to my cell, I asked myself over and over again, *How is this relevant?*

I grew up drawing on everything I could. In elementary school, kids watched as I brought space aliens and other creatures to life. My projects, examples of student creativity, were displayed in the administration building. In high school, I doodled in class, impressed art teachers, and found notoriety by hanging controversial posters.

After graduation, I enrolled in a nearby university where I planned to develop my artistic abilities. But the freedom, friends, fraternity parties, and dormitory life intoxicated me. Overconfident and irresponsible, I studied just enough to get through my freshman year. As a sophomore, I began skipping classes, drinking excessively, trading texts for beer money, doing drugs, and failing miserably. The more I failed, the more I invested in addictions.

Eventually, finding myself so far behind that I would never catch up, much less graduate, I chose a shortcut—lying, cheating, and stealing. This led me in circles until I was hopelessly lost. Facing my own self-destruction was unbearable. Convinced I was powerless, inadequate, and worthless, nothing seemed to matter anymore.

The culmination of my failure arrived with a November 1990 arrest, which led to a lengthy prison term. At age 22, I self-destructed and left a wake of victims behind me. I knew the nightmare wasn't going to go away on its own. I knew I was to blame.

Foreseeing years of prison and living among criminals, I wanted to give up. To try to make myself feel better, I'd look at the other inmates and say to myself, *I'm not as bad as they are. I didn't do what they did.*

But trying to minimize what I had done didn't work. I belonged there and I knew it. The shocking realization came when I asked myself, *Am I one of the worst?* I'd learned the impact of my actions, and every morning they unlocked my cell door, I was forced to face that reality.

The days became numbingly long. When I tired of reading or writing letters, I looked for a pen and drew. Something clicked. I had destroyed my life. Then with a ten-cent pen, I returned to the kid I was years before. I started over, speaking volumes about loneliness, frustration and the hope inside me.

For more than a decade, I painted, drew, cartooned, and illustrated from inside a state prison. Dull hours became precious while the sound of crashing weights, conversation, and card games hummed around me, unnoticed. By building upon the one positive thing I had left, I reinvented myself and felt optimistic again. My work improved and matured, taking on a direction of its own— and so did I.

As my illustrations and paintings evolved, resulting in publication and awards, I found empowerment, confidence, and self-worth.

Prison, a crushing adversity, helped me to realize the best within me. Inspired and moved by the acceptance of who I am today, I feel at peace with myself and those around me. Erased is the likelihood that I will hurt anyone again.

So, the next time I'm in that courtroom, I'll be ready. "Your Honor, I can tell you why I feel my accomplishments are, in fact, relevant."

"Gifts make their way through stone walls."
—*Proverb*

The Spirit of Tuck

Kay Lee

Several years ago, I asked the prisoners that I corresponded with to send me some examples of random acts of kindness. One inmate wrote back, "Kindness . . . in prison? If you think you see an act of kindness in here, you better look behind you, 'cause somebody's setting you up!"

About three months later, I received a letter from the same disillusioned young man stating, "Remember when you asked me about those acts of kindness? Well, at Christmas, a man they call Tuck gave me a box with all these little partly filled bottles of shampoo, deodorant, and nearly a whole bar of soap. These items are precious to us in here. I felt feelings I've never felt before!"

In my first letter from Tuck, he wrote, "I'm trying to change for the better." Tuck was a huge man, only 38 years old, but partially disabled because of medical problems—mostly his heart. It's kind of strange, though, because his heart was huge, kind, and loving. Tuck and I wrote for nearly two years steadily, and I grew to love this big man's spirit.

Letters from Tuck invariably included notes from three or four other prisoners from the same facility. The letters often started out with, "Dear Kay, I never could have sent this letter if it weren't for Tuck giving me a stamp."

Tuck's heart was as great as his physical presence. Every prisoner heard Tuck say at least a million times, "If I'd won the lottery, I'd make sure every inmate here would have $45 a month in his account."

Larry Tucker, an inmate who tried to rise above his past, worked hard to make the present more tolerable. Even with a life sentence, he tried to make the future in prison better for everyone he touched.

Suddenly, in the middle of a dark and lonely night, isolated from help, Larry took his last breath. The entire prison community, including the staff, went into mourning knowing that Larry didn't have a mean bone in his body. His mother wrote expressing her pain. She and I both saw the best in Larry. The prisoners wrote about their loss, "There was never a better friend than Tuck."

[EDITOR'S NOTE: For information on a ministry that encourages inmates by writing to them, contact Romans Chapter 8 at P.O. Box 8771, Endwell, NY 13762 or P.O. Box 1703, Bloomfield, NJ 07003; e-mail: D26TEDDY@aol.com.]

"Every trial endured and weathered in the right spirit makes a soul nobler and stronger than it was before."

—*James Buckham*

Reaching Beyond the Walls

Chaplain George Castillo

*I*t was one of those hectic holiday weekends. The prison camp was overflowing with family members intent on enjoying the last summer weekend with their incarcerated loved ones. Children of all ages were busy playing, running, and pushing each other on the swings at the children's playground.

About 3:00 p.m., I walked the last lingering visitor to the waiting room. As she flung a kiss to her husband, he waved a quick good-bye, turned to me with tear-filled eyes and said, "Chaplain, it is tough saying good-bye to the family." I understood.

A few minutes later, in the quiet of my office, I had a chance to take a couple of deep sighs and praise God that another full day was almost over. Before I could fully inhale the joy of relaxation, a series of knocks at my door destroyed the peace. I opened it, only to face another bleary-eyed inmate who looked close to passing out.

"What's the matter, Bob?" I asked anxiously.

"It's my mother, Chaplain."

Fearing that she had passed, I waited a moment until he was ready to begin talking again. "I've been trying to call her for the last day and a half, and I can't get any answer. I'm worried because she lives by herself and never goes anywhere."

"Has she been ill?"

"Yes. She's 85 and diabetic."

"Give me her number, and I'll give it a try." No answer. Trying to remain calm, I asked, "Do you have any nearby relatives or friends I can call?"

"Mrs. Smith lives across the street, but I don't know her number."

Despite my pleading, the information operator wouldn't cooperate. "Sorry Sir, but I'm not permitted to disclose Mrs. Smith's number. It's unlisted."

My mind kept turning over and over, processing possibilities—then it hit me. My United Church of Christ Year Book. While Bob watched my every move, I thumbed through the pages and located two churches near his mother's home. I called The Reverend at the closest church and identified myself. After emphasizing the importance of the situation, he assured me that he would go immediately to check on Bob's mother. Then I prayed briefly with Bob, as the 4:00 p.m. count was drawing near. He left my office with a glimmer of hope in his eyes.

Within the hour, I spoke with The Reverend again. He shared the good news that he found Bob's mother alive. Before I could get the details, Bob appeared at my door. "Chaplain, I just talked to my mother," he said with a smile. "Church people found her. She was too weak to get out of the tub after her bath on Friday. Thank God, and thank you and all those good people. She's exhausted and a little shaky, but she's going to be okay."

I left the prison camp, two hours after my usual quitting time, feeling grateful that with God and His helpers, I was able to reach out beyond the prison walls to help a distraught inmate and his mother.

An Unexpected Favor

William Ryan

Some of us who have been in and out of prison just don't know where we belong. We continue on the same shady path that leads back to prison. Then one day a little deed comes along to open our eyes and our hearts, making us realize that an act of kindness, a favor done spontaneously in good-faith, can make us feel good. If we help just one person, the smile, the simple thank you can make us feel better about ourselves and the world around us.

I used to think that the greatest "high" came from drugs. Boy, was I wrong. The ultimate "high" comes from surprising people by helping them at the simplest tasks. Now, I'm no Boy Scout or hero, just your average prison convict, but my life was once changed by the simple act of planting a tree.

One fall day, while walking down the street, I saw an elderly lady digging a hole in her front yard. Her tiny, frail body was no match for the huge shovel. I stopped and watched. She wasn't getting very far but she seemed determined to get that tree into the ground anyway.

I walked up and asked her if I could take over. She looked at me in total surprise and disbelief as I dug a generous hole, planted the tree, and gave it a healthy dose of water. Still speechless, she started to smile, unaware that I had recently been released from prison.

When I asked where I could put the shovel and rake, she directed me to a nearby shed. I secured the padlock and handed her the key. As I began to walk away she yelled, "Wait. I don't even know your name."

I returned to her yard and shook her hand. "Name's Bill."

"I appreciate what you did. Bless you, Son. Can I pay you?"

"I can't take your money. I'm just glad I could help out. Promise me you'll take good care of that young sprout now, okay?" Vowing to watch over that young tree, she waved as I continued on my way.

Whenever I walk down that street, I always stop for a moment and remember that day. The simple act of helping that lady gave me a new sense of accomplishment and purpose.

"None of us has gotten where we are solely by pulling ourselves up from our bootstraps. We got there because somebody bent down and helped us."

—*Thurgood Marshall*

The Blind Project

Jerry Gillies

In my first year as an inmate at the notorious Folsom State Prison, I hadn't even heard of The Blind Project. Tucked away in a group of offices and reading rooms at the end of a long corridor on the 2nd floor of the Folsom hospital, 20 inmates and a correctional officer are running one of the most amazing and successful humanitarian projects ever attempted from within prison walls.

Officially known as the Folsom Project for the Visually Impaired (FPVI), it was set up as a community service program in 1989 by the local Lions Club to record books on tape for blind students throughout California. The prison library now has more than a thousand books on tape. By the time I became involved in 2002, the project had dramatically expanded its original focus.

When I first approached Correctional Officer Bob Schmitz, supervisor of the program, about being assigned to the project, I was apprehensive. After all, I would be one of only two non-lifers out of the twenty-man workforce. I worried that they might be hardened convicts who'd be resentful of the new guy. I'll admit I was astonished at what I discovered instead: A deeply motivated group of highly skilled inmates producing large amounts of educational material for the visually impaired, hearing impaired, and disabled community, at a pace and standard rarely matched in the private sector. As a former motivational speaker and corporate trainer, I was struck by the cohesiveness of the group, which could serve as a model for any corporate team-building effort. I'll admit that one of the first things that excited me about my new work assignment was a toaster in our workers' lounge. For the first time in six years of incarceration, I could have my favorite—crispy toast!

What sets The Blind Project apart from every prison program or job I've encountered is the intense focus by these inmates during the workday on activities that have nothing to do with prison life. We are completely engrossed in turning out work that helps deserving people on the outside.

Something else that sets us apart from most other prison inmates is the continuing acknowledgments we get from these outside sources. Letters, phone calls, and faxes pour in from visually and hearing impaired individuals and students, community colleges, state agencies and the like. In fact, one of these letters directly led to the transformation of the project into a multitask, multipurpose entity.

The project began providing books on tape to a blind student named Amelia, a remarkable girl now in high school who has won numerous awards in academics and the arts. Amelia was so appreciative of these otherwise unavailable books being recorded at her request that she wrote a letter in Braille praising and encouraging the inmates. This inspired one inmate serving a life sentence to become the first prisoner in California history to learn Braille transcription, which is now a major part of the program; at this point, sixteen of the project's inmates are certified by the Library of Congress. The California

Department of Education has authorized the project to transcribe a substantial number of textbooks for blind 1st through 8th grade students. With state-of-the-art equipment, the inmates can now publish books in Braille from start to finish.

Cutting-edge computers, software, and equipment also play a part in some of the project's other activities. Closed captioning of videos for the hearing impaired is providing an important service for the state's community colleges. Using a sophisticated electronic gauge, the FPVI inmates are cleaning and gauging the correct prescription for up to 100,000 used, donated eyeglasses, many of which end up in third world countries through the auspices of Lions Clubs International. Several of the inmates have also become experts in the new field of making websites accessible to the disabled, as now required under federal law. They are reaching out to state agencies and organizations helping the disabled, teaching them how to be compliant with this requirement.

One of the most startling accomplishments of this dedicated group of prison inmates is that they are responsible for most of the funding of their own expansion. The sophisticated equipment they use is mostly paid for by grants they have generated by writing their own grant proposals to foundations and corporations. They have even put this expertise to work helping outside organizations. In one case they generated a $126,000 grant that allowed them to purchase a large vision screening van that is used to give glaucoma tests free of charge in the various neighborhoods it visits.

A steady stream of visitors from assorted agencies and organizations come to the Folsom Project for the Visually Impaired. All are impressed by the esprit de corps, the dedication to excellence and the prodigious output of this small group of men committed to serving the visually impaired, hearing impaired, and disabled community. Many of the men have jobs waiting for them with community colleges, state agencies, or the private sector when they are eventually released.

As for me, I am profoundly aware of how blessed I've been to find a place I can spend my days that doesn't feel like prison at all. I love being a member of a highly respected team that serves others and makes their lives better in many different ways. Crispy toast has never tasted better!

[EDITOR'S NOTE: For more information on Lions Clubs International, contact 300 W. 22nd St., Oak Brook, IL 60523-8842; Web site: http://www.lionsclubs.org. For more information on The Blind Project, contact Folsom Project for the Visually Impaired, P.O. Box 16422, Folsom, CA 95763-6422.]

"The greatest tragedy in life is to have sight and no vision."

— Helen Keller

THE IN SIDE
by Matt Matteo

Reprinted by permission of Matt Matteo.

"Learning is a treasure that will follow its owner everywhere.
—Chinese Proverb

2

Daring to Care

"With courage you will dare to take risks, have the strength to be compassionate and the wisdom to be humble. Courage is the foundation of integrity."

—Keshavan Nair

His Brother's Keeper

Cathy Fontenot, CCE

T he year was 1996. He doesn't recall the season, but he will never forget the overwhelming chill that he felt as the corpse fell from the shoddy coffin.

Death is not an uncommon occurrence at Angola. As warden of the state's only maximum-security prison for adult men, it took Warden Cain no time to realize that a majority of the 5,108 inmates would die there. As a result of life sentences, and sentences longer than most people could possibly live, the inmates feared dying alone and being buried on the grounds of the infamous, sprawling Louisiana State Penitentiary.

A simple man with friends in high places, Mr. Cain wanted to be a warden because he saw it as a macho job. After first being given the job of warden at a medium security prison, vowing to do all that he could to keep it, he set out to be his "brother's keeper."

He talked to his mama, a small town retired teacher who opened his eyes, mind, and heart with these simple words: "Son, don't miss your chance to save someone's soul." She reminded him that he could make a real difference in the lives of those men who were not only under his custody, but also, more importantly, under his care. From that moment on he knew what he had to do.

Warden Cain set out to change the hearts of men by establishing moral rehabilitation, which is what he knew to be the only successful rehabilitation. He encouraged men to change their hearts so that they would respect life and know compassion. He was certain that after the men changed their hearts they wouldn't be prone to continuing a life of violence. With new hearts, these men would learn and accomplish anything they wanted to—perhaps even finding hidden talents they never knew they had.

Indeed, Warden Cain became known as the Christian warden. He was known for welcoming thousands of religious volunteers and instituting faith-based programs. The medium security prison he ran worked like clockwork until one day when his boss called. "Burl, I want you to run Angola."

Warden Cain didn't want the job. He knew Angola's wardens didn't stay wardens long. But realizing it was an offer he couldn't refuse, he arrived at Angola in February 1995.

He immediately knew the place was unique. The Warden realized he had fallen away from the moral teachings he had received as a young boy. He held the inmates under his care to God's commandments and knew he had to also follow those same rules. The awesome weight of looking at the men at Angola, who expected a savior in their new warden, caused him to realize he had to fix himself before preaching to them.

"Inmates are just like you and me," Warden Cain points out. "What was important to them before they were inmates is now twice as important. The simple things: good food, good medicine; good playing and good praying; being able to hug your mama; being paid attention to (whether you are being good or bad); and dying with dignity. I knew

I had to make Angola a godly place. Fortunately, most of the inmates wanted the same."

So when the body of one of the oldest inmates fell out of the despicable cardboard coffin, Warden Cain knew what to do to ensure it would never happen again.

Since there were scores of talented craftsmen at Angola, he went to two of the finest carpenters he knew and asked, "How do you feel about building some respectable coffins?" Tears of gratitude welled up in their eyes.

Those inmates, Redwine and Grasshopper, a 70-year-old and a 50-year-old who had worked together for nearly 20 years, made the most beautiful coffins that have ever been seen at Angola. In response to reporters who were fascinated by the prisoner coffin makers, they simply replied, "We make each one with great compassion because we never know which ones will be for us." Once people from the outside got a glimpse of the handiwork, the carpenters began receiving special requests for custom-built coffins.

It didn't stop there. Other inmates, expressing an interest in becoming a part of something positive, built a replica of an antique funeral hearse. Majestic Percheron draft horses were hired to pull the hearse. Warden Cain allowed staff and inmates, who had become like family to the deceased, to attend funerals. Inmate ministers, trained at Angola's in-house Bible College, another program implemented by the new warden, performed the funeral.

Inmate organizations have taken the place of gangs. These inmate groups provide cemetery maintenance workers, gravediggers, pallbearers, and a funding source for funeral wreaths and carnations for each gravesite on special holidays. That's a far cry from the backhoe grave digging days, where only a funeral director and an escorting security person stood to remember the prisoner.

One day, while reading the local paper, Warden Cain

happened across an article on Hospice. Within a year of its implementation, Angola's Hospice became known as a model prison hospice, winning national awards. Inmates volunteered to sit with their dying peers and do everything necessary to make their last days comfortable. Eventually the Hospice Chapel was built, providing a sanctuary for family and friends of the dying. The horrifying fear of dying alone and being buried without dignity no longer gripped the population. There was a sense of security in knowing that many men understood and felt compassion. They had learned respect for life.

So, in 2002, Grasshopper and Warden Cain looked down upon the mahogany-stained pine coffin that held the body of their friend, Redwine. The feeling of warmth from those who came to pay their last respects helped to dry their tears as they dropped on the merciful ground that freed the soul being laid beneath it.

"And the Lord said unto Cain, Where is Abel thy brother? And he said, I know not: Am I my brother's keeper?"
                                                        —*Genesis 4:9 (KJV)*

Watching John

Jerry Gillies

W hen I volunteered for the inmate suicide-prevention companion program, I hadn't a clue that my first night on duty would involve a major shock. I arrived at the prison on the bus from California with John—a short, skinny, beak-nosed thirty-year-old. Since it was the first sentence for both of us, we bonded right away.

Despite his frail appearance, John had been a Navy Seal and had the strength and endurance indicative of intense training. He also had had a bagful of trouble in his relatively short life. He had loved the discipline and adventure of his military life, but it was cut short when he injured his back in a parachute jump. And then his devoted wife died in a car crash. Depressed and broke, John tried his hand at robbing a bank but was caught when a friend turned him in.

Though he acted strange and detached, most of the inmates grew to like John, and no one dared mess with him once they discovered he had mastered several forms of martial arts. He kept busy all the time and hardly slept at all. This behavior disconcerted the correctional officers doing the late night count in our dormitory because John would often be found pacing the floor, covered with a sheet.

Once, a female officer let out a scream when her flashlight illuminated his ghost-like frame, huddled under a desk at the back of the dorm. Another time, he was discovered crawling across the floor, apparently reliving one of his military missions. But John was friendly in a quiet, shy way and seemed to be adjusting well to the daily monotony of prison life.

He earned extra money ironing other inmates' khaki uniforms and spit-shining their boots to his high military standards, often complaining, "The corrections officers' uniforms and boots are so sloppy, they should be put on report!" John liked to talk about his plans once his seven-year sentence was completed. He'd say, "I'll dispose of some property I own, arrange my affairs, and then kill myself."

Few of us took him seriously. We knew a lot could happen in seven years. But he made the mistake of telling this to the prison psychologist, and she decided to put him on suicide watch the very night I began my first shift.

At the back of the prison hospital, down a long corridor, was the suicide-watch room. Larger than a cell, it had a single bunk in the middle. The bunk was bolted to the floor, and nearby was a lidless toilet/sink combination. A small porthole in the steel door allowed for the passage of food trays and medication. Bright overhead fluorescent lights remained on, day and night. A large window allowed full observation of the room from the hall, where a table and chair were set up for the suicide companion.

Companions were invited to talk to the inmate, and when I did, John's first words to me were, "Jerry, this is crazy. I never said I was going to kill myself *now!*" The prison had never had a suicide, largely because of the prevention program, manned by inmates—and the staff weren't about to take any chances.

Equipped with only a sheet, T-shirt, and boxer shorts, John complained that he was cold and bored. Thirty-six hours later, on my second tour of duty (each rotating tour lasted three hours), I brought him a book, a pencil and paper, some magazines, and my handwritten list of "Reasons Why John Shouldn't Kill Himself."

My list included: late night count will be boring without John there to scare the correctional officers; inmates' morale will suffer without boots spit-shined by John; a beautiful woman is out there with weird-enough tastes to fall in love with John; and, no one should die without having at least one more BLT, one more ice cream cone, or one more shrimp cocktail.

John was already laughing when he reached the last item; smiling or laughing at this list proves you still have a few laughs left in you, and it's too soon to go. We both laughed for a few minutes, and by the time I was on watch for my third rotation, John definitely seemed to be in a better mood. We exchanged a couple of letters after he was transferred to a mental health prison facility in Missouri, and then we lost contact.

I served on the suicide-prevention team for another year and sat with a number of inmates. Many were first-timers scared to death of what prison had in store for them. I tried to calm their fears by telling them what to look forward to and how to survive. Others were pretty crazy, barking like dogs, banging their heads against the wall, or zonked out on antidepressants.

But never again did I have to sit and watch someone I knew, and never again did I feel quite as useful as when I was watching John.

"Be an answer to someone's plea. You have a part to play. Have faith. We can decide to risk that He is indeed there, watching, caring, cherishing us as we love and accept love. The world will be a better place for it."

—*Joan Wester Anderson*

"I'd like to volunteer my time to other people...
all 8½ to 25 years of it."

Reprinted by permission of Christian Snyder.

Can I Have Your Autograph?

George M. Roth

T hanks for listening and laughing, and I hope I've helped make a meaningful difference in your lives today. Thank you."

The group of prisoners, dressed identically in white coveralls, rose to their feet while issuing a rousing cheer and hearty round of applause. A friend had invited me to speak to the pre-release program at the state penitentiary. For over a decade, I routinely volunteered my time to a variety of causes. But, as my focus on career and marriage intensified, citing time constraints, I accepted fewer and fewer invitations to speak inside the walls. Even though several years had passed since my last presentation behind bars, I agreed to speak.

Maybe it's the air, stifling even in the absence of humidity. Or perhaps it's the resounding clunk of steel gates slamming closed behind you. I can't say for certain, but once you are surrounded by maximum-security walls, an eerie feeling settles over you; the sensation that you have been swallowed by a building is very real.

Curious friends occasionally asked why, of all places, I volunteered to speak in prisons. Given the strained atmosphere, at times even I wasn't sure why.

Following my short presentation, as I gathered my notes, a smiling young man approached. While vigorously shaking my hand he produced a scrap of paper and hesitantly asked, "Can I have your autograph?"

I was at a loss for words. No one had ever asked for my autograph before. In my mind, people who signed autographs deserved admiration and respect—a view I didn't have of myself. While stammering and searching for a response, the noisy surroundings blurred like slow-motion memories of a car accident, and my thoughts drifted.

The boy was on the scrawny side and came from a family burdened with too many children. Though quiet and unassuming, he was troubled. He worked hard at paying attention in school and even harder at completing his chores at home. Even so, he seemed incapable of meeting the simplest expectations of parents and teachers.

"Why can't you be more responsible like the other kids?" they scolded. He couldn't answer. He didn't know why. Their disappointment cut him deeply. Whenever he felt overwhelmed by circumstances beyond his grasp, his dark eyes slowly glazed over and, like daylight fading at dusk, he would silently disappear into his imagination.

During his teen years he was introduced to beer and, finding its embrace comforting, he drank it at every opportunity. Crippled by the drug alcohol he slid deeper into fantasy until, finally, he was little more than a mind-numbed, dumbstruck bystander watching the parade that might have been his life pass him by.

A decade spun by. The once safe, imaginary world of his childhood was littered with empty bottles, indistinguishable from his nightmares.

Overwhelmed with sorrow and regret, he surrendered to despair. Blinded by hopelessness, he decided to write the final chapter of his disappointing life on the approaching

---

Christmas Day. The birth of a Savior would be greeted by the death of a nobody.

Having settled on an execution date, he breathed a deep sigh of relief. Suddenly, a wrenching wave of sadness washed over him; his body shook and he fell to the floor, sobbing. He curled tightly around himself and whimpered child-like prayers to the God he had abandoned long ago. Finally, exhausted from the strain, he drifted into a fitful sleep and dreamed.

He envisioned a coffin at the front of a dimly lit room. Soft organ music broke the muffled silence; evenly spaced rows of folding chairs sat empty, awaiting mourners. It was his funeral. But in his heart, he knew that no one would bother coming . . .

"... Hey, you okay, Man? How about that autograph ... just trying to give you your propers, ya know what I'm sayin'?" The young man eyed me nervously, still holding out the piece of paper. I awkwardly scratched my name on it and handed it back to him. A broad smile spread across his face and he quietly said, "Thank you."

On a Christmas Day many years ago, my prayers were answered. I experienced a moment of sanity and asked for help. I received hope, understanding, and much more. I learned how to trust, became willing to accept direction, and started building a future. Most importantly, I discovered that, while my life experiences weren't typical, I was not alone.

Over time I achieved a measure of success as an actor, a writer, and a speaker. Out of gratitude for these gifts, I started doing volunteer work. With each new success, and every passing year, however, there seemed to be less time for volunteer activities. Gradually, even though the pain of my past had begun to fade, my appreciation and passion for the present started slipping away.

Some of us need stone walls and steel bars to know the hollow ache of isolation. Others create walls deep within themselves believing that these barriers will shelter them from pain. Whether our walls are concrete or unseen, they are spiritual death traps that leave the soul brittle and withered. Anyone who has endured the anguish of loneliness in a crowded room knows that isolation is a self-imposed sentence that few torments can equal.

Experience has taught me that, given time, isolation will create a foothold for despair. I have seen it in the eyes of frightened cancer patients and felt its suffocating presence among the forgotten elderly. Some times when I speak behind prison walls I sense this cunning specter patiently watching, waiting for me to forget.

Perhaps it is only human nature to want to forget about pain. But the request for my autograph made me realize that the memory of past hurts and the process of overcoming them fuels my passion for living. If I lose touch with my past, no matter my present success, I have no doubt that I am doomed to repeat it.

Today, I know why I speak in prisons—to share my experience and to remember it.

When that young man walked away holding my signature, he left behind the gift of respect. My ego likes to believe that my inspiring words motivated his request for an autograph. The reality is that the positive impact we have as volunteers comes from the simple willingness to share our time. In the eyes of the troubled and lonely it is by our presence that we embody the most powerful adversary of isolation and despair. And that, my friends, is hope.

Can I have your autograph?

"You are not your past. You are who you chose to be in the moment. What you have done does not have to dictate who you are today. You make the choice. When you become your strengths, your personal powers will help you make the right decisions in life."

—*Marcia Reynolds*

Be Kind to Yourself

David Roth

*I*n the late 70s, I worked as a youth counselor in Alaska at a juvenile detention facility. I wasn't much older than some of my "kids." The crimes these young people had committed ranged from petty theft to murder and most things in between—not much room for childhood.

One thing I couldn't help noticing bubbled underneath the surface of their inappropriate behavior: a vibrancy and hunger for trust, structure, continuity, and sense of self-acceptance that they didn't get on the outside. Some came from families who'd moved around a lot; others from small villages where drugs, lack of attention, and boredom were badly combined. Add in peer pressure and posturing, and you don't need a calculator to see what some of the results were.

Years passed, and I gravitated from social work to music. I was in a song-writing workshop one morning and decided to revisit that theme of self-acceptance, sorely lacking in the kids I'd worked with a decade earlier, and that theme's lifelong companion, the inner critic. I gave myself the instant assignment to write some lyrics and, two hours later, I had this song . . .

I have my moments, yes I do,
And I have my dramas just like you.
When the weight of the world comes crashing through,
And I'm needing somebody to lean on.

I look in the mirror and I see
A bundle of nerves where I used to be.
I remember the words you said to me,
The words that you said to me.

"Be kind to yourself, be kind to you.
That's what you're here on earth to do.
If you just let your love shine through,
Then life may be kind to you."

It's easier said than done, I know.
I'm the first to admit I take it slow.
I just have a hard time letting go,
Letting go of the critic inside me.

Some times I prefer to stand and fight.
Then you remind me "Take it light,
Would you rather be happy or be right?
Would you rather be happy or right?"

How can you hope to be helping someone
If your own life is twisted and twirled?
You've got to pull out your broom and clean your own room
Before you can clean up the world.

If I were a master, old and wise,
And people would ask me for advice,
I'd just tell 'em all to memorize
The words that you said to me.

"Be kind to yourself, be kind to you.
That's what you're here on earth to do
If you just let your love shine through,
Then life may be kind to you."

Life may be kind to you.

THE IN SIDE
by Matt Matteo

Reprinted by permission of Matt Matteo.

"Kindness is the golden chain by which society is bound together."

—*Johann Wolfgang Von Goethe*

A Christmas Visit

Debby Giusti

Following a three-year military assignment to Germany, my husband was transferred to Fort Polk, Louisiana, in 1984. Our European tour had been filled with opportunities to help others, and at no time did our outreach seem more meaningful than at Christmas.

Each year we opened our house to the men and women from my husband's unit who were unable to go home for the holidays. To my three small children, the meaning of Christmas wasn't merely Santa Claus or the toys under the tree but the opening of heart and home to others.

As the muggy days of summer shortened into fall, I wondered about the direction of our holiday outreach. My husband's office was staffed with married personnel; everyone had a home to go to on Christmas. But the stockade on post held thirty men who would have no visitors.

A family meeting sealed our commitment, and a call through channels authorized our visit. Eagerly we began our preparation. We purchased gifts: paper tablets, pens, envelopes, and stamps to encourage the recipients to write notes to loved ones far away. Toilet articles, socks, jigsaw puzzles, and decks of playing cards were carefully wrapped by little fingers before being tucked into larger gift boxes.

Their slippery hands greased in butter, the giggling children formed gooey cereal into festive red and green treats. With glee, they wrapped each one in colorful plastic secured with festive bows. Pumpkin bread, baked in individual loaf pans, filled the house with a pungent aroma. Thick chocolate fudge, poured hot into baking pans, cooled into mouth-watering treats.

Pocket-sized New Testaments and Scripture verse cards recounting the birth of the baby Jesus were included, along with our own personal holiday greetings. Then, we sprinkled candy around the gifts before the outer boxes were covered with brightly colored paper and shiny ribbon.

On Christmas Eve, we packed the gifts into our car and left the warmth of our quarters. Riding in silence, we passed row after row of houses outlined with glowing bulbs. The children, usually bouncing with energy and anticipation, were noticeably subdued.

The final path leading to the stockade stretched dark and desolate. The dreary compound, surrounded by a tall fence topped with barbed wire, stood in stark contrast to our cozy, cheerful home.

My husband showed his identification at the guardhouse, and we were given permission to proceed. Without a sound, we gathered up the boxes and entered the stockade. The men stood in formation to welcome us.

As we presented our gifts, my husband and I shook each man's hand, wishing them well, hoping they could feel our compassion and concern. While we filtered through the ranks, the children babbled their Christmas greetings, bringing smiles to discouraged faces.

That simple outreach started a family tradition. The following Christmas other families joined us, and the next year even more people became involved. I don't know if we took Jesus into the prison with us on those cold December nights. I'd like to think we found him there.

And When I Was in Prison, You Visited Me

LeAnn Thieman

I tried not to stare as several dozen female inmates entered the gym one by one, some in white, some in maroon jail suits. A gray-haired woman walked with a cane in small steady steps. A blond with six inches of brown roots patted her very pregnant belly. Another smiled effusively, revealing only three to four teeth. One seemed so young—barely twenty. Her scrubbed-clean face and simple ponytail didn't hide her natural, model-like beauty.

They sat silently, despondently, in the last of four rows of semi-circled folding chairs. "Come on up," Tom coaxed as he walked down the aisle shaking hands with everyone. An Asian girl stared at the wall. A Hispanic woman rhythmically kicked the chair in front of her with her toe. "Here's a front row seat!" Tom beckoned. I watched intently his approach with them. I'd never visited a prison before—never dreamed I would. *So why had I chosen ministering to women in prison as the charity for Chicken Soup for the Christian Woman's Soul?*

I had a feeling I was about to find out.

"How many of you have read *Chicken Soup for the Prisoner's Soul?*" Tom beamed and waved a copy of the book he had co-authored. A dozen women raised their hands. "What was your favorite story?" He pointed to the inmate with a three-inch tattoo on her wrist. "Ivy's Cookies," she said with what seemed to be a rare smile.

I couldn't believe it. There were 101 stories in the book. *How could she have chosen that one?*

"It's one of my favorites, too," Tom said, nearly dancing with delight. "Why is it your favorite?"

"Because this teenage girl took cookies to prisoners like us and they wouldn't talk to her. They treated her all mean and ignored her, but she just kept bringing cookies every week. Then at the end of the story when Ivy is older, one of the prisoner's daughters brought cookies to her at her home. That was so cool." The young woman blushed.

"Well, we have a special surprise for you here today," Tom said. "The author of that very story, 'Ivy's Cookies,' is here with us, and she's going to read that story to you!"

Some inmates smiled brightly at the news while two African-Americans sat stoically.

It was Candy Abbott's first prison visit too, yet she stood in front of them and began reading her story with all her heart. She emphasized how Ivy Jones had questioned herself about why she kept coming to the prison week after week when the inmates clearly didn't appreciate or care about her. Then an evangelist came to the prison and ordered the inmates to make a circle and thank God for one thing. Candy went on to read about the lopsided, silent circle and how one prisoner finally said, "I want to thank Ivy for the cookies. Thank you, God, for Miss Ivy bringin' us cookies every week." Then one by one, the prisoners each thanked Ivy for her weekly visits.

Candy concluded the story and closed the book. "We have another surprise visitor for you today," she said proudly. "Ivy is here!"

Many inmates gasped and most clapped as Ivy walked from the second row to the front of the room. "We've never done this together before," Candy explained.

Ivy reminded me of the evangelist in the story as she addressed them. "I didn't know what I was doing when I was that teenager visiting the prison. I was scared, but I prayed to God to show me what to do and He did. And He'll show you what to do too. Just ask Him!" she proclaimed. "And He'll show you too. If you need strength, ask Him for strength. If you need hope, ask Him for hope. He'll give you what you need just like He did me."

"Amen!" someone shouted.

"God disciplines those He loves." Ivy looked into each of their eyes and added softly, "And He must love you very much."

The model-look-alike's face reddened. She fanned her hand in front of her face as if to wave the tears away.

Ivy completed her brief sermon to the applause of the inmates, and then Tom came forward again. "There is a new Chicken Soup book called *Chicken Soup for the Christian Woman's Soul* and part of the money from the sales of that book will go into a special fund to buy copies of it and *Chicken Soup for the Prisoner's Soul* to give to incarcerated women. We plan to send some to you after the first of the year." A few inmates clapped; many whispered with excitement; some sat motionless, expressionless. "We have a final surprise for you today—the co-author of *Chicken Soup for the Christian Woman's Soul*, LeAnn Thieman." Most of the women clapped with enthusiasm, but a few sat scowling with their arms folded across their chests.

Until that moment I hadn't a clue what I was going to say. I'd trusted God would answer my prayer and give me the words. "It seems we have a theme here today," I began. "Apparently God uses baked goods to help do His work on earth." Some chuckled. Most smiled, except for those with the folded arms. "Twenty-five years ago I bought a dozen cupcakes at a bake sale to help support the orphans in

Vietnam. That's all I ever intended to do for them, but God had a bigger plan. He just used those cupcakes to trick me into helping Him!" In one long deep breath I rattled off my story of how I joined the organization to help support the orphans, how my basement became the state chapter headquarters, how we had decided to adopt a son from Vietnam, how I agreed to go bring six babies back to their adoptive homes, and how, when I got there, I helped bring out 300 as a part of Operation Babylift. The room broke into applause. When I told them the part about a baby boy crawling into my arms and heart and family, a collective sigh filled the gym. "I was not and still am not anybody special," I explained. "I was raised a poor Iowa farm girl with seven brothers and sisters and I wore hand-me-down clothes. I'm living proof that God uses ordinary women to do extraordinary things."

Tom stood behind the group and stared me right in the eyes. "Why did you pick a women's prison ministry for the charity of this book?"

I looked at the old woman with the cane, at the pregnant woman rubbing her belly, at the tattooed woman, and the one with few teeth. I breathed past the lump in my throat. "Because a lot of good is in this room." A tear escaped the model's eyes. The black women unfolded their arms. The Asian woman looked me in the face. I continued. "I know something very bad happened to put you here, but I know you have a lot of good in you."

"Amen!" the voice came again.

Tom hugged me long and hard as I headed for my seat. Then he introduced his wife, Laura, a frequent companion on his prison visits, and co-author of the *Chicken Soup for the Volunteer's Soul* book. "Everybody has a story to tell," she said warmly. "And yours isn't over yet—you can still choose the ending." Many heads nodded in unison.

Tom lightened the mood. "Just like in Ivy's Cookies,

let's all circle up," he cheered. To my amazement, the women followed him to the side of the gym and formed a circle, holding hands. "Now let's say one thing we are thankful for," Tom urged. "I'll start. I want to thank God for letting me be here with you today."

A woman with long graying hair spoke first. "I'm thankful for the people keeping my children strong while I'm in here."

"I want to thank Ivy for coming today—and next time, will you bring *us* cookies?"

"I want to thank Tom and Laura and Candy for coming here today when I'm sure they got better things to do."

"I want to thank LeAnn for donating money from that book so we can get a copy someday. Those stories give me hope."

The model spoke. "I want to thank God for sending me to prison. If He didn't love me enough to send me here, I'd be dead."

"Amen!"

"Everyone take one step forward," Tom instructed and we inched ahead. "Now another step forward," he said with a giggle. "And another." We jammed in closer together. "Now that's a big Texas hug!"

There I stood with my arms wrapped around forty women prisoners, all smiling, all hugging. Indeed, there was a lot of good in that room.

"Each person has inside a basic decency and goodness. If he listens to it and acts on it, he is giving a great deal of what it is the world needs most. It is not complicated but it takes courage. It takes courage for a person to listen to his own goodness and act on it."

—*Pablo Casals*

The Dignity of a Prisoner

Jane Davis

*H*olly and I first met in a women's prison in Georgia. I had gone there to do a story on Jews in jail for the *Atlanta Jewish Times*. Being Jewish, I had never thought about "my people" being in prison. But there they were . . . Holly, Barbara, and others. They had been locked away with virtually no contact with the Jewish community. My "neshama," my Jewish soul, screamed out, "You cannot abandon them!" So I became a volunteer, going through all the training necessary to do prison work. I began going weekly to provide a Jewish connection for the handful of Jews scattered in the prison like prizes in a Cracker Jack box.

Holly was one of the women who came regularly to the group. She had a presence about her, one of confidence, strength and a distrust of newcomers. I knew that I was going to have to prove myself to her—prove to her that I cared and that I was going to continue coming. I sensed that I represented everyone who had ever abandoned her.

Holly had intense eyes that, even behind her thick, oversized glasses, bore through every fiber of any person who happened to be on the receiving end of her scrutiny.

She was thin, about five-foot-five, with a golden mane of hair that was her pride and joy, flowing far below her waist. Holly had no room for games or lies. She had no room for anything but raw, honest communication. If it were otherwise, she would know.

And so began a friendship that lasted many years, both in and out of prison. I looked forward to her wisdom and her sharing. I came to understand that it was her unscrupulous honesty that was disarming at first, but ultimately most welcome.

During her years in prison, Holly had become a Christian. But, given the occasion to reconnect to something that remained alive deep inside her, she welcomed every opportunity to pray and remember her Jewish roots. She held back tears each time we lit Shabbos candles and chanted the Shema—the holiest of Jewish prayers. She glowed in awe when we lit Hanukkah candles, sang Hebrew songs and ate the traditional potato pancakes called latkes.

While she was incarcerated, Holly had some serious medical problems, including breast cancer, from which she never fully recovered. She also developed Crohn's disease, a rare intestinal ailment that disproportionately affects Jews.

One day I received a call from her. "I'm in the hospital," she said. Her cancer had recurred. Holly was so ill that, once admitted to the hospital, she could not return to prison. While undergoing treatments and hospital stays, she lived in the home of another volunteer family.

When I arrived, I could hardly recognize her. She looked as if she had just come out of a concentration camp. Her beautiful hair was replaced by peach fuzz, her cheeks were sunken and her body emaciated.

For a few weeks, I visited her every day. Miraculously, she survived, but her failing body had become another kind of prison. I was amazed at her spirit, her determination and her grace. We didn't talk a lot about why she had been in prison. I knew the details, but that wasn't the focal point of our time together. We spent the time focused on human dignity, love, giving to one another, serving and humor.

One day, I found out Holly had been rushed to the hospital. She was in excruciating pain. Her digestive system was no longer functioning. Doctors told her the only way she would be able to survive would be by intravenous feedings. Holly rejected the idea and treatments ceased.

Her mother came from Wyoming and sat vigil with her. They had not been together for a long time. When Holly finally died, she was surrounded by loving family and close friends.

The first day I walked into that women's prison to write a story, I had no idea that I had actually been led to volunteering my heart and my time.

[EDITOR'S NOTE: For information on a through-the-mail program geared toward individual healing, forgiving and how to use prison time in a positive way, contact Jane Davis, HOPE-HOWSE International, Inc., P.O. Box 9855, Santa Fe, NM 87504; Web site: http://www.hope-howse.org.]

"One's dignity may be assaulted, vandalized and cruelly mocked, but cannot be taken away unless it is surrendered."

—Michael J. Fox

My Friend, Sarama

George Toth

Murderer . . . terrorist . . . killer!" The screams from an inmate a couple of cells away awakened me from a sound sleep. I knew that voice very well, a trouble maker, Lenny.

Only five cells were on the high security max-tier where we were housed, and I called out to Lenny, "What are you yelling about?"

He ranted and raged. "They moved a terrorist in the cell next to me!"

"What are you talking about?"

"They moved one of those 9-11 terrorists next to me," Lenny shouted.

As far as I knew there was only one person at that time in custody in the U. S. for the 9-11 attacks—and that person was not even in our state, let alone this jail. Nevertheless, Lenny continued to verbally assault his new neighbor.

A couple of days later, as I was being escorted to a visit with my attorney, I passed the cell of this alleged terrorist. Being curious, I looked into his cell. All I saw was a sixty-year-old, 110-pound Middle Eastern-looking man with immense sorrow and pain on his face. Our eyes locked for a moment before the officer ushered me to my attorney.

A few days later, Lenny stopped his ranting once the Middle Eastern prisoner was moved. After that, I didn't give either of them a second thought. I had enough problems of my own.

Several months later, Lenny was transferred to another facility. Within hours after his departure, several inmates also moved to different cells, and I was surprised to see the Middle Eastern man again. This time I knew my new neighbor—the alleged terrorist. He still had the same intense look of pain and sorrow on his face. He certainly didn't look like any terrorist to me.

We began to talk through the small window that connected our cages. Although Sarama's English wasn't good, he could get his point across. He always addressed me as "my friend."

Sarama was from Israel's West Bank, and he was Palestinian. He came to the U.S. to visit a daughter who was living here, and while doing so, he made the mistake of taking a job. The money he had earned he sent home to his wife and eight children. Apparently this act violated the law surrounding passport regulations. Sarama had never been in jail before.

It upset me that he was put in jail for working. I understand the pain and sorrow of living in these kennels, but Sarama's anguish was so severe that I just had to ask, "I understand this is not a nice place, but you are way too sad. Why?"

He reached into his pocket and showed me a photo of his wife and children who lived in Israel, all except for the daughter he came to visit here in the U.S. "This is the reason, my friend," he said, tears flowing down his face. "I miss my family. I haven't heard from them in nine months."

My heart went out to Sarama—separated from his family in a foreign country, in jail, with staff and inmates calling him a terrorist. He showed me his paperwork and charges concerning his incarceration. He definitely wasn't being charged with terrorist activity. His charges were exactly what he told me, and according to his lawyer, he would return home to Israel within seventy days. Yet, Sarama had trouble trusting anyone.

Having a good understanding of our judicial system, and after scrutinizing his paperwork, I reassured him, "You'll go home soon. No more than seventy days."

His eyes sparkled at this revelation, but I could sense he still couldn't believe it, especially after all the taunting, which seemed to lessen when they placed him next to me. Everyday, I assured Sarama that he would be with his family soon; yet I worried that before then he would die of a broken heart.

Before Sarama moved to our unit, he lived in an isolation cell for seven months, with no human contact except those who fed him. Although he fasted and cried out to Allah all day long, he didn't eat much of the food they offered because it didn't conform to the Islamic criteria.

We became close as the days went by. He told me stories about his family, Islam, and the Middle East. He gave me lessons on speaking Arabic, and in return I shared stories about my family and America. I taught Sarama some Spanish and English, and together we read the Holy Bible and discussed Scripture.

Although I tried to give him a glimmer of hope and ease his pain, each day Sarama continued to cry for his family. When he prayed to Allah, I prayed too—not for me but for him. I wondered, *How could a man be thrown in jail for honest labor?* I just couldn't understand it.

One morning a correctional officer came to Sarama's door, ordering him to pack his belongings. Immigration was there, waiting to send him home. The smile on Sarama's face permeated the whole unit. He looked into my eyes and said, "My friend, you were right. I *am* going home. I will never forget you. I love you, my friend. You are the best thing that happened to me in America, and I shall tell my family about you every day."

"I'll write to you, Sarama . . . so you won't forget me," I laughed.

As the officials began to take him away, Sarama asked the CO, "Before I go, may I hug my friend?" This was an unusual request, certainly unheard of and definitely off-limits here in maximum security. Lucky for us, the correctional officer that day was a kind man who had spent time at my tray slot, conducting Bible studies with me.

Without a word, the officer unlocked the door to my cell, and Sarama walked over to me. As we hugged, he uttered, "Allah Akbar."*

Choking back salty tears, I said, "Allah Akbar." I watched them walk down the corridor until they were gone.

My friend was no terrorist. Sarama was a hard-working husband and father who had unconditional love for Allah and his family.

---

*God is Great.

"A friend is one before whom I may think aloud."

—Ralph Waldo Emerson

Something Worth Coming Back To

Michael Bowler

As a long-time volunteer in Juvenile Hall, I can testify to the fact that almost every boy there lacks a decent role model, a respectable man to emulate, someone to show him a better way or simply to give him some time.

Pablo, one of the most frightening boys I've ever met, was a puny 14-year-old who shot another boy three times to steal a backpack he never really wanted. Pablo had the unnerving habit of giggling throughout his court proceedings, most notably when the court-appointed psychiatrists declared him to be a sociopath.

When I first met Pablo in the High Risk Offender Unit at Juvenile Hall, I knew none of this, but he was only too happy to tell me all about it. In fact, his only regret was that his victim survived to testify against him. Pablo was a hollow boy, who seemed indifferent about his mother, his sister, and even his girlfriend. "If they were killed today," he said, "I could care less!" His chilling words were delivered in an empty, dispassionate tone, accentuated by that creepy giggle. He was like a teenage version of Hannibal Lecter. And yet I sensed something in him—something beyond words, buried deep down inside. So I kept going back, week after week, just to spend an hour with him.

He talked about being alienated from his mother, his long-departed father, drug abuse, gang affiliations, and lack of friendship or love. The conversation was usually one-sided whenever we discussed feelings. Pablo didn't appear to possess any. I just listened and continued to be present for him.

His case dragged on for a year but finally, at the age of 15, he was convicted as a juvenile and sentenced to ten years in the California Youth Authority. As the date of his departure from Juvenile Hall approached, I detected an uncertainty in Pablo, totally out of character. Even his giggle lost its edge.

I talked with Karen, the only other volunteer who spent time with him. "Pablo seems different to me," I said. "I think he'll miss us."

"No way!" Karen responded emphatically. "He still gives me the creeps!"

"He promised to write."

Karen sighed, "Don't hold your breath. That boy doesn't care about anyone."

After eight months passed, I began to think maybe she was right. Then, out of the blue, a letter arrived addressed simply to "Mike and Karen." The short note read: "Hi, it's me, Pablo. Just letting you know I'm doing okay and not getting into too much trouble." He signed it and sketched a little picture. Beneath all that, larger than the rest, he wrote an enormous letter "I." Then he drew a little heart, the letter "U," and the word "people." My heart skipped a beat as I read his message: "I love you people."

Never, in the entire year that I'd known him, had I heard the word *love* pass that boy's lips—not once. Maybe the word was so foreign to Pablo that he had to draw the heart. But the emotion was there. We had touched him after all.

In later letters, Pablo asked me why I kept coming back to spend time with him when everyone else had given up. I told him I saw something good in him. I had sensed the real human being hiding inside because I had seen, deep within him, the face of God. He never stopped thanking me for that—for believing in him when no one else did.

Pablo changed. He excelled in every program they threw at him, and through the years, he established a loving relationship with his mother. After graduation day, he sent me a photo of himself in cap and gown, hugging his mom and waving his prized high school diploma. In fact he did so well, the administration allowed him to take his SATs on the outside. While incarcerated, he applied to and was accepted into college.

Released earlier than anticipated, Pablo is now 25 and studying at his local university. He's doing well, and he attributes much of his redemption to the fact that I kept coming back. As he said, "You made me realize that there must be something in me worth coming back to."

"Example is not the main thing in influencing others. It is the only thing."

—Albert Schweitzer

THE IN SIDE
by Matt Matteo

Reprinted by permission of Matt Matteo.

Who in your life do you need to forgive? Who do you need to ask to forgive you? Make a list of these people. Then call or write to each person to ask for forgiveness or forgive him or her. Don't just say, "I'm sorry." Instead ask, "Will you forgive me?" or say, "I forgive you." Remember to look in the mirror, and look into your own eyes and say, "I forgive you, and I love you."

—Tom Lagana

3

Liberating Forgiveness

"Life consists of choices. We can choose forgiveness and to see the divinity in each person. This choice gives us a fulfilling life."

—George Castillo

Total Truth

Tom Lagana

*F*orgive my family and friends? No way," Rob growled. "I'm going to hurt them when I get out of here!" These angry words came from one of the inmates who had agreed to participate in our Alternatives to Violence weekend workshop.

"You're missing the point, Rob. This exercise is designed to help us learn how to express our anger and work on ways to forgive," another inmate replied.

Rob's body language matched the intensity in his voice. "I did everything for them," he snarled, waving his arms as he spoke. "Since I've been in the joint they've done nothing for me. I'm going to hurt them," he insisted, "even if it lands me back in here!"

As the workshop progressed and small groups rotated, mixing up the interaction, Rob repeated his story. During the breaks, I could hear him talking the ear off anyone who would listen, trying to justify his threats of revenge. "They let me down. As soon as I get out of here, I'm going to get them back," he boasted. Despite the group's efforts to help Rob see he would only end up hurting himself by clinging to his resentments, he refused to let go of his destructive thoughts.

On the last day of our weekend behind the razor wire, we were instructed to sit quietly and write a letter to someone with whom we were angry. This particular exercise, called "The Total Truth," was an important part of the intensive experiential workshop. Rob squirmed in his chair throughout the exercise. His biggest problem appeared to be selecting one particular person that made him angry from a comprehensive inventory of grudges.

The beginning of the letter consisted of an in-depth description of our anger and resentments. The subsequent paragraphs were devoted to explanations of our hurts, fears, regrets, and wants. The focus of our writing in the closing paragraph was on forgiving the target of our animosities. Actually mailing the letter wasn't a requirement, but writing it down was essential for a successful outcome to this exercise.

After the 30 minutes were up, everyone pulled their chairs back into a large circle to discuss the benefits. As I glanced over at Rob I couldn't help but wonder, *What ridiculous made-up excuses will he share?*

As we went around the circle, each volunteer and inmate took a turn sharing. We discussed insights we had gained from writing our letters, including ways of applying this technique of addressing anger and finding forgiveness and appreciation of self and others to our daily lives after the workshop was over.

Throughout the discussion, Rob's behavior was out of character. He remained silent. The exercise was about to come to a close when Rob took a deep breath and cleared his throat, apparently ready to speak. I braced myself for the fury I had come to expect from my bitter acquaintance. As he spoke, the evidence of the healing power of forgiveness (amplified by everyone in the circle) had found its mark.

We were rendered speechless as Rob spoke. "Looks like I have a lot of people to forgive and plenty of letters to write." In the end, he had spoken the total truth.

[EDITORS' Note: See page 195 for "The Stages of The Total Truth." For information on Alternatives to Violence Project (AVP), see Web site: http://www.avpusa.org.]

Reprinted by permission of Christian Snyder.

"Anger is a momentary madness, so control your passion or it will control you."

—Horace

The Surrogate

Teresa Tyson

My story began in Mexico on May 5 (Cinco de Mayo), 1992. I was raped and almost murdered at knifepoint in Chiapas by a young Guatemalan man whose mother had been killed in front of him by American soldiers when he was seven years old. Thankfully, with a lot of inner spiritual work and the help of a therapist, I was able to forgive him by August of that year and go on with my life.

In January 1997, I was invited to attend an Alternatives to Violence Project (AVP) workshop at a maximum-security prison in New York State. AVP comprises a series of experiential three-day workshops on creative, non-violent conflict resolution.

On the second day of the workshop, I discovered that rapists are at the bottom of the prison hierarchy, just above pedophiles. One of the younger inmate participants was ranting on about the despicability of rapists when I felt moved to speak. I had told my story to victims, to conference participants, and to church congregations, but I never thought that I would ever speak to offenders about my experience.

At first I tried to shrug his words off, but as he continued to denigrate and belittle rapists, the feeling grew stronger. I looked over at the woman facilitator who had invited me. She knew my story. Silently, we communicated with our eyes. I needed to speak. She knew and agreed.

When the participant finally finished, I asked permission to speak. "I don't want any of you to misunderstand what I am about to say, but I feel the need to say it. A few years ago, I was raped and almost murdered at knifepoint. I am not excusing what he did. It was absolutely inexcusable, but that doesn't mean it is unforgivable. For me those are two different things."

The room grew silent. I felt all eyes focus on me. "Just because someone does something horrendous doesn't make him a horrible person. Their action means they made a mistake." From the silent, expressionless faces, trained solely on me, I couldn't tell what effect my comment had on the group.

As I sat wondering what I had done, chow time was called. As the men rose to leave, a very muscular inmate seated next to me in the circle said in a barely audible whisper, "You've got a big heart." Then he left with the other inmates except for the AVP inmate facilitators who were allowed to eat with the outside visitors in a nearby office.

As soon as I finished eating, a very tall, heavy-set inmate facilitator came up to me and asked if he could speak with me privately. Because privacy doesn't exist in a maximum-security prison, we went out into the hallway. The nearest correctional officer was about 20 yards away. Because of the inmate's eloquent, intellectual dialogue, and the way he presented himself, I assumed he committed a white-collar crime and belonged to the

15 percent of inmates at this prison serving time for non-violent crimes. When we reached the hallway, he turned towards me, sighed deeply and began to wring his hands. "I don't know if I can do this," he said quietly.

"It's all right," I said. "Go ahead."

By this time his face was beet-red but still he continued softly. "This is so hard . . . I can't do it . . . I have to . . ."

After waiting in silence, wondering what he would say next, I encouraged him to continue. "It's okay. Whatever it is, say it."

He swallowed a few times and then took a deep breath. "Would you be a surrogate for me for a moment?"

I knew what a surrogate was, but I had no idea what he meant. Since I felt safe, I answered, "Yes."

Tears began to flow down his cheeks as he spoke. "A long time ago . . . I hurt a woman VERY VERY badly. I've tried to apologize to her family, but they want nothing to do with me. I respect that. I don't want to hurt them any more than I already have. I just want you to know how . . . how deeply sorry I am for what I did." Then pausing to catch his breath he added, "And for what was done to you."

I was speechless, watching this gigantic man trying hard not to fall to pieces in the middle of the corridor. I held his gaze and, after a moment or two, he whispered, "Do you think you could forgive me?"

Now it was my turn to take a deep breath. "Yes," I said. I wanted to hug him, but I knew touch was taboo, so I continued to hold his gaze. After a few seconds he blushed and asked, "May I hug you?" I nodded, and we quickly embraced before joining the others in the office. Thankfully, the correctional officer apparently didn't notice the hug.

In those few moments, time stood still. I wondered, *How many years has he waited to say this to someone? How many thousands of other men and women in prison are waiting for someone to listen to their pain and their heartfelt apologies?*

I was overwhelmed with a feeling of "coming home." Although I had long ago forgiven the man who raped me, he was never apprehended. Yet now I was sharing the healing power of forgiveness with another. As I looked at this man, I knew that I would become an AVP facilitator and do this for the rest of my life. I had finally found my "calling."

Three months later, I returned to complete my AVP facilitator apprenticeship on the same workshop team with my surrogate.

[EDITOR'S NOTE: For information on Alternatives to Violence Project (AVP), see Web site: http://www.avpusa.org.]

"The weak can never forgive. Forgiveness is the attribute of the strong."

—Mahatma Gandhi

Where Love Is, God Is

Joan Wester Anderson

S ister Maurella Schlise, a Catholic nun from Fargo, North Dakota, had served others in many ways, primarily as a teacher and a hospital chaplain. But never as a prison visitor. Not until one Christmas when she traveled, as she usually did for the holidays, to the Florida home of her sister and brother-in-law, Rosemary and Pat Ryan. The Ryans had started a prison ministry, conducting weekly nondenominational prayer meetings at a nearby maximum-security penitentiary.

No more than thirty-five men ever attended, but Rosemary and Pat refused to become discouraged. If prayer lifted these prisoners out of despair and regret for just a little while, allowing them to focus on the One who loved them despite all they endured, the hours Rosemary and Pat donated were well worthwhile.

Visitors were never allowed to bring anything to the prison, not even food. But when Sister Maurella arrived at the Ryans' house, she found holiday food preparation in full swing—not just for the family but for the prisoners too. "Because our regular prayer meeting falls on Christmas Eve this year, the prison officials decided we could bring each of the men a few goodies," Rosemary explained to Sister Maurella. "We're going to make some Rice Krispies bars and homemade cookies for them. Enough to fill about fifty bags."

"Fifty bags! I thought you said turnout was pretty low," Sister pointed out.

"It usually is. But maybe on Christmas Eve, some extra men will come. We wouldn't want to run out. Besides, for most of the inmates, this will be their only gift."

Sister was glad she had arrived several days early to help with preparations. Rosemary obviously had even more to do than usual.

The following morning Sister attended mass. She thought about the inmates, wondering if they—if anyone—could actually experience the miracle of Christmas from behind bars. What would it be like? Then, "Although God is not in the habit of speaking directly to me," she says, smiling, "I distinctly heard a voice in my spirit. It specifically said, *Bring one hundred bags of candy and cookies to the prison.*"

One hundred! It seemed far too many for this small group. "I thought it might be my imagination," Sister said. "But I decided to step out in faith and tell Rosemary and Pat about the Voice."

Rosemary and Pat were skeptical. But they too had had experiences when God seemed to "nudge" them just a little, and they respected Sister Maurella's insight. If Sister were wrong, the worst that could happen would be leftover bags, and plenty of places could use extra sweets at Christmas.

The women spent Christmas Eve doing many chores, as well as filling one hundred white bags with homemade treats and candy. After dinner, they loaded the car and drove to the prison gates. The guard waved them through. Sister Maurella looked around. *So this was what a penitentiary looked like.* Someone was hurrying toward them. "That's the chaplain," Rosemary explained.

"The chapel is filled!" the chaplain called. "I've never seen it so crowded. There must be a hundred men inside!"

A hundred! The women smiled at each other. That little nudge from heaven had been real, after all. How glad they were that they had acted on it and prepared extra food.

Pat carried the box of white bags into the chapel, planning to begin the meeting in the usual way. But the prisoners had a surprise for them. They had prepared their own Christmas program.

An inmate with a vibrant voice sang the moving story of the "Little Drummer Boy." Another performed the "Ave Maria," having somehow discovered that it was one of Rosemary's favorites. Everyone sang hymns, and one man read the Christmas story from a battered Bible. The chapel was hushed, small candles providing the only light. It was truly the most poignant Christmas Eve service that Sister Maurella had ever attended.

Finally the program ended, and the men eagerly lined up. Sister and Rosemary handed each a white bag. "Thank you, Sister; thank you, Miz Ryan," they murmured . . . until ten men were left in line. But the bags were gone. One hundred had not been in chapel. One hundred and ten were there.

One hundred and ten! Sister Maurella was distraught. If God had truly spoken to her, why hadn't He told her to bring one hundred and ten bags? What should they do? *God, multiply the bags,* Rosemary prayed silently.

But a young convict had also seen their dilemma. "Sister," he spoke quietly, "we'll share our bags with them."

Sister Maurella looked at the faces surrounding her. Men of every color and nationality; murderers, thieves. But men who now, because of Christ's birthday, were willing to reach out to one another in forgiveness and love. Healing sometimes came in tiny steps, Sister knew. But once begun, it could grow.

The young convict opened his bag, preparing to divide his sweets. Just then, a prison trustee entered the chapel, carrying a sack. "Rosemary, we had some leftovers from a group that came this morning," he said. "Can you use them?"

Rosemary took the sack. Inside were candy and cookies, divided into ten white bags.

The group was astonished. "You see?" Rosemary smiled as she handed the bags to the remaining men. "Our God loves us so much that he cares for us in even the smallest ways."

Everyone, especially Sister Maurella, rejoiced as the ten men received their treats. She had wondered if Christmas could come in a prison, but now she knew. Where love is, God is.

[EDITOR'S Note: Originally published in *The Power of Miracles, Stories of God in the Everyday.*]

"If we pray, we will believe; If we believe, we will love; If we love, we will serve."

—*Mother Teresa*

The Circle

Danny Edward Scott Casalenuovo

Three years ago I was arrested for impersonating a police officer. No, I wasn't behind the wheel or even on a two-wheeler with blue and red flashing lights. I was stealing from private homes in broad daylight. I didn't steal because I needed the money. I stole for the sheer thrill I got.

As I entered the Los Angeles County Jail, the cruel reality came crashing down on me, piercing my heart. I was leaving my beloved and devastated family behind. My wife and daughter were forced to move in with my in-laws. At the time of my crimes, I was the sole provider. My wife was forced to stand by and watch our home, our car, and our family life slip out of her grasp.

I alone caused the foundation and security of our home and a beautiful life, as well as my child's future, to crumble. I created fear in both their lives and caused much destruction because of the horrible choices I'd made. A year and a half went by before my wife started writing to me. Those 18 months were hard on her and our daughter. The shock of it all continues to upset their lives today. But the events leading up to my arrest tell only part of the story.

My new home was no longer a four-bedroom house vibrating with the laughter of a child giving hugs and smiles. My new home was dark and empty without my loving wife who brought beauty and light to my every day and so generously gave from her heart—the love, warmth, and trust that transformed our house into a home.

My new home didn't have a glowing fireplace with crackling logs, the inviting aromas of a home-cooked meal, or a sweet daughter to tuck in at night and read a bedtime story to. My new home didn't have a front porch. I could no longer sit on the swing with my wife and have a nightly calm-down talk under a billion brilliant stars. Gone was the bond of trust and comforting closeness of my wife and daughter—the two people I love most.

My new home was a musty, square jail cell—a dingy, depressing room with dull gray paint peeling away from the walls like a bad sunburn in summer, and big, brown, armor-plated bugs crawling out of every corner. Three hundred and fifty men lived in that giant concrete tomb—each with an unstable attitude ranging from anger and hate to greed and lack of self-control.

The day I first walked into that stale cell, my only possession was tucked under my arm—a blanket. I was wearing the rest of my capital. One pair of socks, a T-shirt, jumpsuit and one pair of much-too-small boxer shorts because processing wasn't the time to be choosy about sizes.

All the bunks were occupied, so I scouted out a spot on the floor, away from most of the traffic and chaos, and moved in. I rounded up a foam-mat and made house with my blanket. Exhausted and emotionally drained from sixteen hours of being herded through like cattle, I collapsed onto my bed.

The following day, a short, slight man awakened me. "Would you like a book to read?" To this day, I still don't know his name.

Looking up at him, I mumbled, "Sure . . . thanks."

That was the day I was fortunate enough to receive a copy of *Chicken Soup for the Prisoner's Soul.* During the days and weeks that followed, I read it from cover to cover scores of times. I read that book so many times I could recite some of the stories as if they were favorite poems. And I wouldn't be exaggerating if I were to say I think of these stories as my daily Bible reading.

One day, a nearby inmate asked me what I was reading. "Oh, I'm sorry," I said. "I didn't realize I was reading out loud."

This old man stared at me with a look of intense interest before he finally said, "Would you start that story over and read it to me out loud?"

At first I was embarrassed, not knowing how to respond. Suddenly, "Sure I will," fell out of my mouth. I proceeded to read "Strangers Behind Glass" to Old Man Sam. A great change took place in my heart that day. A fulfilling happiness, some kind of peace surrounded my spirit—my soul.

As I read that story to Old Man Sam, I saw deep emotions reflected in his eyes. A chain reaction occurred at that moment. I found myself crying with this stranger who was now my new best friend. It was a wonderful release, a tremendous feeling to share so deeply with a stranger.

Within the hour, Old Man Sam had rounded up seven buddies. They, too. were much older than me. In no time, Sam had me reading stories to them. Within 30 minutes, I was crying right along with those men.

What's happening? I thought to myself. Each of them were finding genuine honesty—real men sharing real emotions with one another within the filthy, uncaring chaos—without being judged for releasing their tears. In fact, most were the strongest in that cage—a concrete warehouse of 350 souls.

As days passed, the group, now known as "The Circle" grew from seven to fifteen. Some of the faces changed. Those who were no longer there had either been sent off to the bigger "houses" or released. Newcomers took their places. As I looked around at the group, I noticed the mixture of ages. And then I saw a familiar face. Old Man Sam was sitting right next to me.

My readings continued, and daily that circle of men sat quietly for two full hours. During those readings we could escape the madness and hatred that thrived around us. Every once in a while I'd look over at Old Man Sam, and he'd release a big, beautiful smile.

One of our reading sessions had to be cut short because of an important announcement. The housing deputy declared, "Canteen will be delivered this evening to those who ordered earlier in the week!" Immediately a great change took place. I'd never seen grown men act in such a way. Most of the men I'd been reading to, including Old Man Sam, were involved in the confusion. Men scattered around like giant ants.

Every jail or prison has a crowd of tough guys—I call 'em "weak bullies." Just about the time all the confusion begins, the bullies surface. These tough guys caused the confusion.

As I sat back and paid extra attention to my surroundings, I tuned in to what was taking place. Each of the bullies was conducting serious business with many of the older inmates. Some of those being bullied were from The Circle. One was Old Man Sam. As I observed, I noticed the bullies were taking the identification wristbands from the older, defenseless guys—some of whom were mentally and physically challenged.

A big ruckus erupted in a far corner. Old Man Sam had just been dismissed—his wrist naked. As The Circle regrouped, I realized what was happening. Their heads hung low, the bare-wristed men stared at the floor, withdrawn—some cried. Sensing fear and tension, I waited for a few moments. I didn't know what to say. "Where are your wristbands?" I looked at Sam, waiting for an answer to confirm what I had pieced together. Then I noticed a red hand print tattooed on his left cheek.

"Who slapped you Sam?" As my words registered in his mind, Sam raised his left hand to cover the welt on his face. In tears, he looked at me and said, "Don't ask!" Then he arose and walked off, followed by half of The Circle. Filled with anger, I planned my next move.

When the canteen arrived, Old Man Sam's name was called, but he didn't move from his bunk. Instead, the bully who had stolen the wristband answered to Sam's last name, made his way to the front of the crowd and collected two plastic trash bags full of supplies, after first showing his band. Then he casually walked away.

Next, a giant of a guy, passing by without a word, dropped off the wristband on Sam's bunk. As Sam slipped the tattered band back over his bony hand, he rolled over and faced the wall. At that moment I realized what an awful time those people must have had. Innocent people having their homes invaded, their personal belongings stolen. What anguish I'd caused those victims! What I'd done was very wrong!

I couldn't watch the madness any longer. Running to the front of the dorm, where a deputy stood observing the canteen distribution, I let the cat out of the bag. As the next bully approached, I tipped off the deputy to what was taking place. When that tormentor advanced to the front to collect what was not his, he was checked, busted, and taken away. After an emergency count, the deputy knew that what I'd told him was true. Each member of The Circle was reassigned to a safer housing unit. At least three dozen men moved out—including Old Man Sam. Deep into the night, nine thugs wanted to have a "talk" with me about my ending their "Fund Circus." When they were done, I reported to the front of the dorm in dire need of medical attention.

X-rays showed a broken right hand, fractured right wrist, shattered right cheekbone, and broken nose. What the x-rays couldn't find, my nerve endings pointed out. But through all the pain, a great smile lay within my heart.

Soon after I was casted and bandaged, I too was reassigned. Wouldn't you know it? The first face I saw was Old Man Sam and most of The Circle. They couldn't believe my condition—neither could I. I was most upset about the fact that I'd lost my book. *Chicken Soup for the Prisoner's Soul* helped me spiritually—it fed my soul.

Old Man Sam knew how I felt and suggested I wing it. So, from my memory, I recited some of the stories that touched me deeply—"While You Were Out," "If You Will Welcome Me" and "A Wise Old Man." The Circle grew quickly to twenty. Although I felt naked without the book that I'd grown to love, The Circle enjoyed my recitations.

Then, close to Christmas, we had just begun to tell personal stories about our lives when a curious movement at the front of the dorm interrupted us. "Someone just moved in," we heard. I recognized a familiar face from the gray dorm—the monster that had broken my hand and blackened my eyes.

"Oh God!" I yelled. Reaching into my locker I grabbed a razor and concealed it in my left palm. I was ready to protect myself through a second round. The mountain of a man walked right up to our circle and looked into my eyes. He stood in front of me for what seemed forever. I uttered, "What?"

"It took a lot of courage to do what you did."

"No!" I said, "What I did was the right thing. It had to do with being a good man. Have you come to beat on me some more?"

Staring down at me with sinister eyes, he reached behind his back. When he brought his hand back into view, he said, "This belongs to you. I saw you reading it. I found it the night I hurt you and now I want to give it back." Handing me my book, this giant man apologized. Standing there in silence for a few seconds, he continued, "Do you mind if I join The Circle? I'd like to listen to you read."

I was shocked! Not only because he'd just asked me if he could join us, but also because I was willing to read to him. The ten minutes that followed were the strangest of my life. Many changes were taking place within our hearts.

As I sat there, dumbfounded, with blackened eyes, a casted hand, and a nose that throbbed to every beat of my heart, I opened my book to the story "My Bag Lady Friend and Me" and began to read aloud. The opening quote by Hubert Humphrey told me what I needed to hear at that moment: "The greatest healing therapy is friendship and love." Reading further into the story, I noticed a change taking place in the giant's features and posture. Something seemed to be causing pain in his heart. With a sad, worried look, he slumped forward in his seat. I continued to read and the giant abruptly stood up and interrupted. "Name's Allen. . . I'm sorry for hurting all of you . . . and stealing from you."

What Allen did that day helped all of us, especially me. I began mailing out apology letters to my victims. In those letters I wrote a little about what had happened in the Los Angeles County Jail and how Allen's words led me to send my apologies.

When I got a response from one of my victims, I was surprised. I wasn't expecting to receive anything in return. In his letter, the writer expressed his thanks and then added the following statement: "It seems your life has come full circle, and you've become a victim of your own crimes."

That couldn't have been truer. I'm sorry for my wrongdoings. Today I do everything I can to help others— within the law. I do my best to bring a smile to someone's heart and go out of my way to lend a hand.

I love life and all it has to offer. To continue living as a radical would be a waste of a good person. I've learned from my mistakes. Today I'm moving forward, full of smiles and hope for a beautiful future—not only for myself but also for my beautiful wife and daughter. I'll be the daddy that she needs, and the man I'm supposed to be for the wife I love.

Two days after the evening Allen sat with The Circle, I was transferred to prison. So I suppose I'll never know what became of all those wonderful-hearted men, including Allen. It took courage to do what he did. That evening, Allen apologized personally to each man he had abused. He even gave each one a hug.

The Circle of men became so addicted to hearing stories from my book every day, that when it came time for my transfer, I decided to leave that wonderful book behind. It belonged with the hearts of many and was intended to be read daily, to those without hope. When I handed that book to Allen, he vowed he'd read from it. He also promised to find someone who would read it out loud.

Before I left, Allen was already at work making a cover for it. *He'll take care of it,* I thought. *And he'll take care of the wonderful hearts all around him too.* I left that jail smiling.

THE IN SIDE
by Matt Matteo

Reprinted by permission of Matt Matteo.

"When I read a book I seem to read it with my eyes only, but now and then I come across a passage, perhaps only a phrase, which has a meaning for me, and it becomes part of me."

—W. Somerset Maugham

Another Mother's Son

Mary G. Lodge as told to Laura Lagana

When my beloved 18-year-old son was murdered in 1996, I thought my life was over. When it finally sunk in that this vivacious child of mine was dead, I felt as if I were having a heart attack from head to toe. I was numb. In order to survive this twisted nightmare, 1 moved to a different level of consciousness.

During the trial, I wasn't allowed to speak to Robbie's murderer. On the day of the hearing, I got my first glimpse of Shawn. He stared at the floor as they led him into the dimly lit courtroom. Shadows masked his face, distorting his features, giving him a grotesque, fiendish appearance. Although it was my decision not to take the stand, I made it clear to the judge that I wanted to speak with this evil perpetrator after his sentencing.

At the conclusion of the arduous proceedings, the judge summoned me to his chambers. Filled with rage and hatred, I followed the bailiff into a small, paneled office. My heart beat faster with each step as I prepared to meet the young man who took my son's life. Shawn stood in the corner, head down, crying like a baby. His hands and feet shackled, this trembling, pitiful 20-year-old wore little more than baggy orange prison garb. As I watched this boy, so forlorn—no parents, no friends and no support—all I saw was another mother's son.

Suddenly I found myself asking, "Can I give you a hug, Shawn?" He looked up, revealing a childlike face stained with tears and nodded his consent. The bailiff motioned me toward the prisoner. I walked over and put my arms around him. "I forgive you for this horrible thing you've done. I will pray for you every day that you're in prison. I would rather my Robbie be where he is than where you're going." Our eyes connected for a few moments, and then the bailiff escorted me from the room.

Shawn received a 20-to-40-year sentence. How do you compare that to the life of my son? No sentence could bring Robbie back. I still wonder what made Shawn commit this crime. He has given me several explanations, but I still don't have an answer. He has been in prison for five years now, and, so far, I'm his only visitor. Shawn's sentencing has given me no satisfaction, but I believe the compassion I felt in the judge's chamber that day was a gift from God.

Because of the abrupt changes in my life, I'm now part of a prison ministry. I know I could not heal the deep, dark places of hatred and revenge imbedded within my heart and soul had I not forgiven my son's murderer. Forgiveness has set me free.

Hatred and revenge won't bring back my beloved son, Robbie, but Shawn is someone's son too. The hatred has to stop somewhere. What better place to begin than with me?

"God pardons like a mother, who kisses the offense into everlasting forgiveness."

—Henry Ward Beecher

The List

Toni Carter

He is a living fountain of love who nourishes the souls around him. Out of what appears to be nothing, he gives everything. He doesn't own a home. He doesn't own a car. He doesn't even own a suit or a pair of dress shoes. And yet, he demonstrates so much abundance by giving all that he has to others.

Blake is a blessing for the incarcerated men who wouldn't normally have the opportunity to hear a motivational speaker. He serves those who have fallen from the favor of family and friends and those who have come to believe that life is a bleak and dismal experience that must be endured.

For more than ten years, Blake has given three motivational talks each week to groups of men in a California state prison. Clear thinking and upbeat, he inspires the inmates by his words. Even the roughest of the bunch readily concede that Blake has a way of touching them.

One such character was "Cowboy." Blake told me about Cowboy because he just couldn't figure him out. He described Cowboy as a nefarious looking character who sat in the back corner of the room seemingly lost in his own world. He didn't talk to anyone other than his "boys." He rarely uttered a word—grunted mostly. With a roving eye and distrustful scowl, Cowboy gave the impression that he was determined not to let anyone or anything penetrate his finely crafted emotional armor. But Blake knew that appearances could be deceiving. And the very nature of prison demands some sort of manly protection.

Keeping a positive attitude, Blake continued to do what he did best and prayed that those who needed to hear the message would hear it. Then one day, a miracle seemed to happen.

Some of Blake's words about forgiving others fell on Cowboy's ears and sank into his brain. Blake spoke about how holding on to grievances and resentments spreads poison through our own bodies and how forgiveness was more for us than for the other person. "Forgiving frees us so that we no longer feel like we are carrying a dead mule. For every vengeful, unforgiving thought, that mule weighs a pound heavier," he said.

Blake had no idea of the importance of his message until a week later when Cowboy sought him out. Cowboy hollered, "Blake!"

Blake froze in his tracks. He couldn't imagine what Cowboy wanted with him. Blake turned around slowly to find a grinning Cowboy standing in front of him, without his boys. "After that talk you did a few nights back about forgiving, I went back to my cell and tore up a list of names I'd been holding onto for years."

"What names?" Blake inquired.

"The names of folks who done stuff to me. Folks who snitched on me and some who didn't come to help me when I thought they shoulda. They all hurt me in some way."

"Wow!" said Blake, "You really tore the list up?"

"Yep! You got to me with that talk about the weight I was carrying and that nobody cares about it but me."

"And how do you feel about not having a list?" Blake continued.

"It feels weird 'cause I thought it was my job to get even with everybody. I'd been holdin' on to that list and lookin' it over every week for the last twelve years. Without it, I feel like I done put the mule down." Then Cowboy gave Blake a big hug.

The list is no more. In its place is a lighter heart. That day, Blake touched one of the roughest of the bunch.

"One of the best places to start to turn your life around is by doing whatever appears on your mental 'I should' list."

—Jim Rohn

4

Acting with Compassion

"Our task must be to free ourselves from this prison by widening our circles of compassion to embrace all living creatures and the whole of nature in its beauty."

—*Albert Einstein*

Covering Kids' Backs

Mary V. Leftridge Byrd

A couple of weeks ago, I saw a woman out in the street on a very cold and windy night. She was trying to button a coat that was obviously too small—one she'd clearly never be able to button. I watched her and felt touched by what I perceived as misery.

While I wept about her circumstances, my mind quickly moved to think of children who had no coats, or coats that were too small, too big, or permanently stained from being handed down too many times.

When I went to bed that night, I couldn't get her out of my head or my heart. When I thought about it again the next morning and got to my job as a prison warden, I met with a group of inmates representative of our population—older, younger, diverse, short-timers, long-timers and men who have so much time to do, they can't see the end of it. I presented them with the idea about kids being cold. I called the inmates and staff together, and we raised more than $2,400—enough to buy 130 coats, mittens, and hats for children in the cities of Chester and Philadelphia.

The clothing was stacked up in our conference room—boys' coats, girls' coats, babies' coats, snowsuits—red, blue, brown and green, corduroy, nylon, polyester and wool, with hoods and without. We had so many—I'm talking layers and layers—that they had to be heaped on my credenza and chairs.

The room looked like an elves' workshop. Literally hundreds of staff and inmates gave from their pockets, experiences, and hearts to make this happen in eight days. It's one of the most remarkable things I have ever witnessed in my twenty-plus years in corrections. I can only lay claim to the *idea* of covering kids' backs. The inmates and our staff are the ones who made it happen.

What a blessing it is to be part of this prison community that values having a soul as much as it appreciates the count clearing. Our prison is a place of which to be proud. And, trust me, I am proud every day, even on those days when I wonder if I should have pursued the only other career that ever interested me. But there isn't much call these days for a mature Warden/Interior Designer.

"In spite of often harsh circumstances, terrible isolation and apparent hopelessness, I found caring, humor, compassion, and yes, even love, expressed by some of the most hardened of my fellow offenders."

—Matt Bader

Checking In

Steve C. Hokonson

On Christmas Eve 1993, another chaplain and I walked the tiers of our prison. That day we weren't ministering in our typical pastoral way—counseling and praying with inmates. In contrast to the blustery, arctic cold outside, the stifling, stale air inside was especially overwhelming by the time we climbed to the fifth tier of a 250-man cellblock.

We barely paused at each cell as we hurried along. With a cheery "Merry Christmas," we placed a six-pack of candy bars on each cell door. Some acknowledged the confection, some slept, and some shouted a strident, "Thank you!" as we sped by.

Although our arms were tired from hauling cases of chocolates up and down stairs, we knew we had done a bit of walking by the time we finished giving six candy bars to all 1,400 inmates. We have never done it since, but that year we had extra money in our Chaplain fund.

Inmates never forget. In fact, they're still talking about the year the chaplains gave out candy bars.

When I came back to work after Christmas 1999, I found an envelope in my mailbox, addressed to The Chaplain. Inside was a check for $150 made out to the

Chaplain Fund, dated December 24, 1999. No letter, no note, just the check. Curious, I called the telephone number on the check to thank the benefactor. When I asked him why he sent the check on Christmas Eve, he said, "Because six years ago you were there on Christmas Eve."

"They were only candy bars," I responded.

My generous sponsor replied, "But you were there for me on Christmas Eve."

After a few more words of gratitude, I hung up and glanced at the check again. It was from a company that he owned.

"Everyone needs to be valued. Everyone has the potential to give something back."

—*Princess Diana of Wales*

Angel Tree

Terrell L. Thomas

*T*hose who want their children to get a Christmas present may submit an application and talk with an Angel Tree volunteer." The surprising announcement, which blared over the loudspeaker, immediately brought conflicting thoughts to mind. *I'd love to give gifts to my children, but they live three thousand miles away . . . and I have four of them. What kind of presents would they be anyway—socks or a cheap plastic doll that keeps losing its head?*

Despite my uncertainty, I filled out the form and on the space set aside for a personalized message, I wrote, "Daddy loves you."

By the time Christmas arrived, the cold reality of confinement had crept in, and I'd become preoccupied with feelings of remorse and self-pity. I'd all but forgotten the pleasant surprise intended for my kids until Christmas day when I called my family.

My wife shouted, "Daddy's on the phone. Hurry and open the presents he sent."

In the background I heard the furious ripping and rustling of paper and joyful exclamations, "Just what I wanted!" and "I can't believe they let Daddy out of jail so he could get us presents!" Each of my darlings received not one but two wrapped gifts with my special greeting. And, unlike the cheap toys I'd expected, they were the latest, most sought-after toys.

Compassionate Angel Tree volunteers reached out and touched my family and me, replacing despair, disgrace, and doubt with trust, hope, and love. That Christmas we also received the precious gift of human kindness.

[EDITOR'S NOTE: Angel Tree is a part of Prison Fellowship Ministries. For additional information, see Web site: http://www.prisonfellowship.org or contact a prison chaplain.]

"We are each of us angels with only one wing. And we can fly only by embracing each other."

—Luciano de Crescenzo

Another Peanut Butter Sandwich

Charles W. Colson

When she arrives at the prison gate each weekday at noon, the guards wave her through. Prison officials stop to ask how her kids are doing or about her work at the office. After all, Joyce Page is family; she's been spending her lunch hour at the St. Louis County Correctional Institution just about every weekday since 1979.

Joyce began going to the prison with her supervisor, also a Christian concerned for prisoners. When the supervisor was transferred, Joyce continued by herself, leaving her office alone with a peanut butter sandwich while other secretaries bustled off in clusters toward the cafeteria.

Each day Joyce meets with a different group of inmates, from the men in isolation and maximum security to a small group of women prisoners. "What we do is up to them," she says. "Sometimes we have a worship service, or a time of testimony and singing, or in-depth Bible study and discussion. How we spend our time depends on their needs."

When she slips back to her desk at one o'clock, one of her coworkers is usually already bemoaning her lunch time excesses and loudly proclaiming that she really will have the diet plate tomorrow. Joyce laughs to herself. She knows exactly what she'll have for lunch tomorrow—another peanut butter sandwich at the wheel of her car on the way to prison.

For many, meeting with inmates every day in the middle of a hectic work schedule would be an unthinkable chore. Joyce, in her matter-of-fact way, sees it differently. "For me it's a real answer to prayer," she says. "You see, I don't have time to go after work—I have six kids of my own that I'm raising by myself."

[EDITOR'S NOTE: For information about Prison Fellowship Ministries, contact a prison chaplain or see Web site: http://www.prisonfellowship.org.]

"It's not how much we give, but how much love we put in the doing—that's compassion in action."

—*Mother Teresa*

A Time of Pain: A Time of Love

Ray McKeon

*T*his story began when I received a message from the Baptist chaplain. He left a name and cell number on my answering machine with the message, "He's Catholic. His mother just died, and he can't go to her funeral. You need to see him real soon. He sounded desperate."

David, a twenty-nine year-old prisoner, had just tested positive for HIV, and his mother had recently died in a shelter. He was empty and hopeless. While on probation, David went back to the hotel room his mother shared with a boyfriend, to retrieve her personal belongings. David discovered that the boyfriend's relatives had moved in and the personal effects were gone.

When he spotted one of the boyfriend's relatives outside the hotel, David became angry and started a fight. Grabbing the other man by the collar and gold neck chain, he threw the man onto a parked car and threatened bodily harm if his mother's things weren't returned. The manager called 911.

The police arrived to break up the fight. When they discovered that an out-of-control David was on probation for robbery, they booked him. Since the gold chain broke free during the struggle, he was charged with assault and attempted robbery.

Facing five years in prison and maybe even a life sentence for violating the conditions of his probation, plus an HIV diagnosis, David became despondent. He was on the seventh floor of the Hall of Justice while his mother was downstairs in the Coroner's refrigerator, without the benefit of a religious service to mark the last transition of her life.

I listened to David for about ten minutes. His dilemma seemed so impossible. To be allowed to go to a service, he would have to pay two deputies to accompany him—yet he couldn't even afford a telephone call.

"The prospects for a funeral seem dim," I said. He began to sob—gut-deep and filled-with-pain type sobs. When one of the other inmates placed his arm around David's shoulder, I felt like a fool. Resolving to do everything in my power to find a solution to his dilemma, I assured him, "I'll be back tomorrow to let you know what progress I've made."

Walking out of the cell-block, I suddenly remembered the address of the hotel where his mother had stayed. Images flashed through my mind as I recalled having been there myself. It was poor—tough, alcoholic, drug-dealing, pimping, scrounging, dirty poor. Even a bleak jail cell seemed better in comparison. I said a quick prayer in my mind, *Please, God . . . help me to help David!*

I hoped to find a friend in the Senior Deputy's office. We had worked on problems together before. At least I would find out what I couldn't do. My friend filled me in about David's past experiences. Resolving to speak from my heart, I asked, "Should a man be denied permission to attend his mother's funeral just because of his past?"

The Senior Deputy, a nice guy, squirmed in his chair. "No, I guess not," he responded. "But how will he come up with the money for the deputies and the funeral?"

"If we get a volunteer priest to preside at a service, we wouldn't have to move David at all," I ventured. "If the service were downstairs in the Coroner's office, we could classify the process as a prisoner-movement." A wild idea soon turned into a proposed solution when the watch lieutenant joined in.

Could we find a priest willing to do the service for free and get the Coroner's approval? I called Father Louie, a good soul who loves the poor, knowing instinctively that I could count on him. Although a solitary service at the county morgue wasn't one he looked forward to, he graciously agreed. With the coroner's consent, the problem was down to a simple act of ministry—a time for David, his mother, and God.

During the brief service, two armed deputies sat outside the viewing room door. David struggled to be strong as he stared at his mother, under the shroud, behind the glass. He loved her dearly. This was a mother who had spent ten years in prison. After her release, she rescued David and his brothers from abusive foster parents. Now, at age fifty, she was gone.

A tearful David stood silently in his orange sweats, leg irons, belly chain, and handcuffs. Father Louie solemnly covered David's mother with the sheet, followed by the embroidered white shroud that almost covered the red tag on her toe. In that moment I prayed that God would welcome David's mother home and guide him through the realities of losing her, returning to prison and life with HIV.

David and I never discussed what took his mother's life. She wasn't able to give David much of a start, but she gave him what she had, and he was grateful. They loved each other. Then it was time to say goodbye.

"We can cure physical diseases with medicine, but the only cure for loneliness, despair, and hopelessness is love. There are many in the world who are dying for a piece of bread, but there are many more dying for a little love."

—Mother Teresa

THE IN SIDE

by Matt Matteo

Reprinted by permission of Matt Matteo.

"There were nights I quietly sobbed myself to sleep—only to awaken and find nothing was different."

—George Barnes
Inmate

They Call Her Granny

Shelly Currier, RN

The first time I met Granny, I was being oriented to the nursing position at the county jail. Even though I am involved in prison ministry, I had never worked as a paid employee in the correctional system. I was nervous. The county jail, designed to hold approximately 150 adult inmates, male and female, currently has more than two hundred inmates. Those incarcerated here are serving sentences for misdemeanors or are being held, pending trial, for serious felonies up to and including first-degree murder.

Granny was seated at the nurse's station in the medical department. She was receiving report from the nurse coming off duty. Granny had a well rounded figure, cream colored skin and wore thick-rimmed glasses. Her gray hair jutted out from under the red and blue scarf she wore on her head. Detecting an accent, I later learned she was from Oklahoma. I listened to the report given by the nurse regarding those who had received medical care. Granny spoke to the nurse in a soft, sweet voice that conjured up images of a grandmother reading a bedtime story to her grandkids. She knowingly nodded her head as report was given on each inmate and periodically made comments in order to provide me with some insight as to their medical problems.

My supervisor told me to observe Granny as she performed her duties that first day. By the end of the shift I was totally overwhelmed by the myriad duties and responsibilities that came with this position. Granny assured me that once I'd learned the ropes and established a routine, I would do just fine. She was right. I've been at the jail more than a year now, and I actually enjoy caring for the inmates. More importantly, I've come to admire Granny.

Granny is several years my senior but has a vitality I can't match. She loves working the evening shift which I, along with most of the nursing staff, consider to be the busiest and most difficult shift at the jail. I've watched Granny set up evening medications, sometimes for as many as 80 inmates, in about thirty minutes. This job takes me anywhere from one-and-a-half to two hours to complete. By memory, she knows what medications the majority of inmates are taking. Granny is so proficient that if a randomly selected handful of pills were thrown on the table, she could tell you the name of each pill as well as the reason it was to be administered.

She is also unique in her ability to screen sick calls and get to the core of most inmates' medical concerns to ensure they get proper care. Needless to say, she is a health care advocate for the incarcerated, ensuring inmates' health care needs are met. But this talent in itself isn't what makes her special. You could probably find nurses working in prisons all over the country with these same talents. The quality that makes this lady so special and has earned her the title "Granny" is her compassion.

Only Granny can shake her finger in mock chastisement at some of the most hardened of men and elicit a smile and their promises to behave. I've often heard her say,

"Now look at this beady-eyed old woman, and listen to what she has to say." Those eyes are anything but beady. Granny's eyes are bright, and they don't miss much. They become tear-filled at times because her empathy and compassion for others has genuine depth. I've observed her conversing with troubled inmates, offering fitting scripture verses to help them through their difficulties. When asked, she even prays with them.

On occasion Granny is severely limited due to back pain from chronic arthritis. I've watched her stoop down, ignoring her own discomfort, to clip the toenails of an inmate who was unable to perform this task and too timid to tell the guards or nursing staff. This same man has been incarcerated for almost a year, awaiting trial. He spends 23 hours a day in his cell in the medical department. Granny received permission to make copies of crossword puzzles so he would have something to occupy his time—a small gesture that meant the world to this individual.

In the past, many inmates have been disappointed by nursing staff who promised to take care of a particular problem and then failed to follow through. Staff members' intentions may be good, but the demands of the work schedule may not allow adequate time. I've learned that keeping one's word is very important to the imprisoned. Granny never forgets and, as a result, has earned the prisoner's trust.

One evening, an inmate was placed in a filthy cell with a horrible stench, despite vehement protests. Granny called the supervisor and requested the cell be cleaned without delay. The supervisor told Granny the cleaning could not take place for some time. It seems the trustees who performed the cleaning had to wait until a guard could be present, and the guards were occupied elsewhere. Granny was furious. The inmate, who was on a suicide watch, was becoming increasingly agitated. As expected, Granny used her charisma to get the job done immediately.

The inmates started banging on their doors and shouting in support of their fellow inmate. This kind of behavior can quickly evolve into an ugly scenario, but in her soothing voice, Granny quieted the potential storm. "I appreciate your concern, but I've got a handle on this situation. Now I want all of you to calm down and behave."

The inmates responded, "Yes, Granny," and a hush fell over the unit. The trustees arrived shortly thereafter, accompanied by a cleaning detail. The matter was resolved just as Granny had promised.

I experienced firsthand the power of this woman when she joined hands with me in prayer at the nurses' station. As she took me in her arms and gave me a big hug and told me she loved me, I felt her warmth and compassion. I've seen that love and compassion flow from her—not only to me, but also to the inmates entrusted to her care. Yes, the definition of compassion can be found in the dictionary. It can also be found at the County Jail in the form of a sweet, gray-haired nurse whom we lovingly call Granny.

"If nothing is going well, call your grandmother."
—*Italian Proverb*

Kindness
Comes in Small Packages

Laura Lagana

My first trip into a prison as an official visitor was with
my husband in the deep South—to a maximum-security
men's facility. Tom and I had been cleared weeks prior to
our July visit.

After showing our driver's licenses and passing through
metal detectors, a correctional officer escorted us through
multiple sets of steel gates. The razor wire glistened in
the sun like gargantuan skewers in a barbecue pit. We
walked under the blistering sun into a cavernous concrete
building. A sudden chill ran down my spine. Guards
observed all movement through ceiling-to-floor windows
from strategically placed elevated stations. Finally we
reached the visiting room, equipped with small clusters
of wooden tables and chairs, much like my elementary
school classroom from yesteryear.

We met and greeted one of our gifted contributing
authors for the first time and began talking. I couldn't
keep myself from glancing around the room every few
minutes. On my left was an affectionate middle-aged
couple. They held hands and smiled at one another
throughout their visit. To my right was a jovial group
of seven folks, including two bubbly youngsters about
seven or eight years old. As they exchanged laughter and

repartee, obviously savoring their family reunion, I mused, *This could be any family enjoying a festive outing, a pleasurable picnic or an unforgettable birthday get-together in another setting—beyond the razor wire.* And straight ahead was a distraught young couple. Continually interrupted by a playful toddler, the willowy man seemed to be trying to sort out something serious with the woman seated next to him.

Our tables were situated about five feet apart, close enough to be seen but distant enough not to be overheard. Officers circulated regularly among the tables, keeping an eye on things, making sure the visitation was proceeding without incident and according to regulations. Near the end of our visit, the troubled young man broke down in tears. With the baby now in his lap, he held hands with his lady; all three were crying outright. When I looked up again, I saw a circulating officer slow his pace just long enough to deposit a small packet of tissues onto their table as he passed by.

After bidding our friend a fond farewell, we filed out of the room with the rest of the visitors. The little girl and boy, who only minutes before were filled with joy at their party, sobbed and tugged on their mother's arm. As they were reluctantly towed from the room, their impassioned, agonizing cries echoed throughout the hollow passageway. "Daddy . . . Daddy . . . I love you Daddy!" Through the glass and steel door they waved and watched as their father was led through a door on the far side of the visitation room to a waiting chamber where he would be strip-searched before returning to his cell.

As I watched those children, I wondered, *How will they remember their childhood? Where will they be when they're my age?* I felt grateful to have had the security and loving discipline of both my parents when I was young. But I was even more grateful to see that kindness is alive and well, even in maximum-security.

Abundance of Love

Joan K. Johnson

As parents, most of us believe that losing a child through death is the worst-case scenario. But I know from personal experience that there is another worst-case scenario—to lose a child to prison.

My own son was one of those kids that got hooked on drugs—permanently. The nightmare started during his last two years of high school and continued into young adulthood. Jeffrey managed to stay clean and sober for about nine months at a time—tops. Convinced that he would always have only this kind of life, he turned to a life of crime to support his habit.

When he was finally caught and convicted, my son entered the Texas prison system for the rest of his life. I didn't know anyone who had ever been in prison before.

Shortly after Jeffrey's conviction, an acquaintance asked me about my family. As I choked on my unusual answer, "My son is in prison," I could see the uneasy look in her eyes as she cut the conversation short and hurriedly walked away. Suddenly, I felt the stigma associated with an incarcerated loved one. Although most people didn't want to deliberately close me out, they couldn't overcome their feelings.

As a long-time volunteer in our church, the PTA, and other organizations, I knew support was available to me. Remembering a discussion about prison ministry during my volunteer work with Cursillo, I called a few people that had worked with me on that Christian weekend. To my disappointment, no one had a recollection of who might know about the prison ministry.

Feeling desperate and alone, I stopped by a church that I once attended. At the coffee hour after Sunday service, I was greeted by someone who was eager to hear what my children were up to. For once, when I mentioned that my own son was in prison, I saw a genuine look of hope.

The woman put her arm around me as she explained, "My husband is working at a Kairos weekend in a nearby prison, and I'd be happy to have him call you after he returns. Is that okay?"

Relieved that someone had finally understood how I felt and unable to speak, I simply nodded.

"Good. John will be in touch. God Bless!" She smiled and waved as I walked away in tears. I was grateful that she reached out to help me in my time of despair.

The following week, John called. "My wife, Brenda, told me about your visit to our church. Have you ever heard of Kairos or Kairos Outside?" he asked.

Clearing my throat, I answered, "I'm familiar with the word Kairos."

"Well, it's a three- to four-day weekend that surrounds the inmate with love, forgiveness and understanding," John continued. "The devoted volunteers go into prisons to work with people who have a willingness to change their lives. Are you interested in helping out?"

My mind wandered. *Here is a way for both Jeffrey and me to survive this ordeal. People are giving their time and love to help make life more bearable for inmates and their families.*

As we talked, John promised to see if the program would be available at Jeffrey's facility. "There's a Kairos Outside Weekend coming up in three weeks. Would you like to go, Joan?"

Kairos Outside supports women who have loved ones who are or have been incarcerated. Being a steadfast volunteer myself, I assumed he meant as a volunteer. But as we talked, I discovered that John really meant as a guest. "I don't know," I responded with trepidation. "I need time to think about it."

"Fair enough," John said. "Let me know when you're ready."

Even though I had been hurt by others who didn't want to associate with me, I asked myself, *Am I ready to be in a room with other women who share my plight? Aren't I different?* I was looking for someone who would accept me—someone who would understand my feelings. *Most of these women probably feel the same way I do,* I surmised.

So, I went to Kairos, where I felt more love and understanding than I had ever known. Living with the shame and embarrassment of having a loved one in prison is a disheartening journey—a journey far too difficult to experience alone.

After my weekend, I made a commitment to volunteer in the Kairos Outside ministry. I went there to find someone I could talk to, and I left knowing I would always have an abundance of love to turn to.

Those gentle volunteers made it possible for me to live through a double tragedy—two worst-case scenarios. Not only did I lose my own son to prison, but I lost him a second time when he died there. Many people stood by me through the painful days that followed. Without the volunteers from Kairos Outside, I would never have been able to survive the journey.

[EDITOR'S NOTE: Contact Kairos, Inc. at 130 University Park Drive, Suite 170, Winter Park, FL 32792 or their Web site: http://www.kairosprisonministry.org]

5

Awakening the Spirit

"If there is light in the soul,
There will be beauty in the person.
If there is beauty in the person,
There will be harmony in the house.
If there is harmony in the house,
There will be order in the nation.
If there is order in the nation,
There will be peace in the world."

—Chinese Proverb

Ode to a Six-Digit Number

Sandra Milholland

*E*very workday morning I leave behind the refuge of my home for life behind bars. And, like most prison employees, I have a love-hate relationship with my job. I love being a woman of integrity in an unstable environment, and I hate having intimate knowledge of man's inhumanity to man.

Prison is a paradox in every respect. It is a study in contrasts, like a picture negative where white is black and black is white. Perpetrators cry "victim," and men who have exploited the rights of others in society now, as prisoners, demand to have their own rights protected.

Prison may be the closest thing to hell on earth, but God is there, too. I know this paradox to be true because I've seen Him time and time again—in white, in gray, in street clothes.

As I drive to work under blue West Texas skies, I watch a morning dove take flight and herds of cattle graze contentedly in fields nearby. This pastoral scene offers a temporary peace in contrast to the atmosphere in prison that awaits me. Prison is dangerous. If I let down my guard or become too comfortable, I can get hurt.

A large sign supported by rough stone reads, "Texas Department of Criminal Justice—Institutional Division." I turn in and steel myself for whatever challenge awaits me. On most days, I pass an ocean of men in white, wielding hoes called "aggies." Dozens of human "chains" strike the earth to different beats, as the wind carries their chant. "Hoe, hoe, hoe, step! Hoe, hoe, hoe, step!"

An officer on horseback, armed and watchful, touches the brim of his hat and gives a formal nod. Given another time and place, he might smile and say, "Good morning, Ma'am," but we both know he dares not do so now. Smiles are a sign of weakness in this environment.

I have met and counseled thousands of men in prison, but I want to tell you about just one. He could be any man or woman behind bars. He did his time as a six-digit number, but he was a human being created in the image of God who deserved to be respected as an individual. As a prison therapist and a Christian, I was supposed to help him change his perspectives on life, but paradoxically he helped me change mine.

Looking back, I can see what a contrast we were. He was Legion and I was a Pharisee (Luke 8:26-38). He had lived a painful life. Crime, self-abuse, and neglect had left their scars. His jumbled speech and empty eyes betrayed the early stages of dementia. Fearing he had murdered one of his victims, out of remorse he poured gasoline over his body and set himself ablaze—an act which explained the missing fingers on each hand.

Wearing my fine clothes and best therapeutic expression, I listened as he described how cocaine and heroin had seduced him. How he habitually traded food for drugs, and how he had been in and out of jails and mental hospitals most of his life.

After he left my office, I remember thanking God for the privilege of working with men like him. *Jesus walked with men like him,* I mused, and *Jesus talked with men like him. What a blessing to be able to do the same.* I felt proud to be working in the trenches where others feared to tread. I was so smug.

Then the Spirit got my attention. My self-righteous attitude turned to shame as I remembered *I am just like him. I am no better, no more loved by God, and no more deserving of the joys of our Creator than this man or any other human being—behind bars or in "the free." There is only one difference between us—I have hope.*

Two weeks later, he died violently in prison, never knowing how our brief encounter would affect my life—and now yours.

Prejudice and pride are not kept behind prison walls or razor wire. They run wild all around us and steal our freedom to be light in a world of darkness. When I remember that man, I see the face of God, and it jolts me to my knees.

"It may be a mystery—indeed a paradox—that all that is noble about the human spirit, its capacity for love, selflessness and compassion, sometimes emerges in the least likely of places."

—Matt Bader

THE IN SIDE
by Matt Matteo

Reprinted by permission of Matt Matteo.

"We must accept finite disappointment, but never lose infinite hope."

—Martin Luther King, Jr.

Amazing Grace

Ken "Duke" Monse'Broten

Grace was married and going to college while working as a correctional officer at our state pen. A beautiful young lady with long curly hair, she was one of those people who just made me smile meeting her. She had the ability to disarm even the toughest old cons with her humor and made us want to protect her.

After our evening meal in the prison chow hall, my friend Mac and I were walking to the cell block area. I lit a cigarette and Mac got on me about it. "Duke, ya gotta quit smoking. Those things are gonna kill ya," he said. I'd heard the same lecture from Mac many times over the years.

Mac was a real health fanatic. He lifted weights and had the body to prove it. He also ate wheat germ and devoured vitamins by the handful—and, of course, constantly complained about my smoking.

My answer to Mac was always the same, "I know it, just shut up. You're worse than my ex-wife." Mac would laugh, punch me in the shoulder, and we would do it again next time.

This night, Mac told me his neck was bothering him. He thought he might have pulled a muscle lifting weights.

After I finished my cigarette, we went our separate ways—Mac to his assigned cell block and me to mine.

A few hours later, an excited watch commander rushed into my cell, asking for a phone number for Mac's family. He explained that they had found Mac on the floor of his cell—dead of an apparent heart attack.

I asked the watch commander if I could go and see my friend one last time. The commander told me it was okay with him as long as it was okay with the medical people.

Walking into D-block seemed strange. Five tiers high and 40 cells long, it was normally noisy to the point of a roar. Now it seemed almost spooky quiet. The wing sergeant told me the medical people were done with Mac's body and that it was locked in the cage at the rear of the cell block.

As I walked down the long, silent tier, I stopped at my old friend Curly's cell. Curly was sitting silently on his bunk, in tears. Moving his finger up to his lips and motioning for me to be quiet, he whispered, "Listen." After a few seconds I heard muffled singing from the cage at the rear of the cell block—like someone trying hard not to be heard. I could barely make out the familiar strains of "Amazing Grace."

When I got up to the cage, I could see my friend's body lying peacefully on a stretcher. And over in the corner, singing in muted tones as she stood guard over my friend's body, was Grace.

I stood there for a few seconds, said a prayer, and left quietly. When I passed Curly's cell on my way out, he whispered, "Grace." I nodded my head, and we both looked at the floor. I don't know if we were saddened more by what death had done to our friend, Mac, or by what his death was doing to Grace.

The First Four Pages

Marcus Cater

*H*e often sat on "death watch" with dying prisoners. The inmates at Snake River fondly called him "Duke." With enormous hands, gray hair, and a battle-scarred face, he carried a tattered, taped-up old Bible—the pages yellowing, wrinkled, and worn. I knew of him from word of mouth.

Duke read his old Bible to men on their deathbeds— it made no difference to him whether they were awake or not. He'd read to them right up until the end. Volunteering his time to do this made him feel better.

One day, I noticed that a number of pages were missing from Duke's old Bible. When I asked him about it, he just smiled and said, "Some Hippie probably ate those pages," and with a laugh he dismissed the subject.

A few weeks later, I had an occasion to watch Duke read to a dying man named Bill. He told stories, laughed with him and read from his Bible. When Bill finally died, I saw Duke tear off a piece of one of the pages from his Bible and place it over the dead man's heart. Then he put his great hand over Bill's heart and said a prayer of thanks to God.

Not long after that I saw Duke walking around the prison yard. I asked, "How many men have you read to until they passed away?"

"Thirty-five . . . fifty maybe . . . not really sure."

I laughed, telling him what I had seen. "Hey Duke, no hippies ate them first four pages . . . or any of those other missing pages neither."

Duke kinda laughed. "You know, I don't know why I do that. I guess it's because I want the men to take a piece of this old Bible to a better place. If people were to find out they'd probably think I was nuts." As he turned to walk inside, he added with a smirk, "Well, the cat's out of the bag now, I reckon."

"Two prisoners whose cells adjoin communicate with each other by knocking on the wall. The wall is the thing which separates them but is also their means of communication. It is the same with us and God. Every separation is a link."

—*Simone Weil*

Legal Advice

Dave LeFave

Arrested for the first time, I found myself sitting in jail on Cape Cod for armed robbery. At nineteen, I knew nothing about the law, but I did know I was facing a serious charge. The court appointed me a public defender, but I had very little faith in him.

A fellow inmate told me about an elderly man who came to the jail every Tuesday afternoon to volunteer. A retired attorney, Bob offered free legal advice and encouraged a Christian lifestyle.

I had my first visit with him one afternoon, hoping to get some competent legal advice, but I got so much more. Soon I began to see Bob every Tuesday, just to talk. Before long, we formed a bond.

Eventually I was found guilty and sent to prison. Bob and I wrote to each other regularly, and occasionally he came to visit. He continued to go to the jail and volunteer his free legal advice, right up until the day he passed away. Since he touched my life in a special way, I dedicate this poem to Bob.

To an elderly man who volunteered for a job,
A gentleman I'm proud to call a dear old friend: Bob.
He taught me many a lesson, not found in many a book,
About the love you can find if you know where to look.

In my new world of darkness, Bob held up his light,
Giving me guidance and courage to fight.
As I slumped in a jail cell, arraigned for my crime,
Bob entered my world, donating precious time.

This elderly stranger, so caring, so nice,
Offered both friendship and legal advice.
He'd help draw up motions, good advice dispense.
And by his example show the Lord's presence.

Although it was clear we were generations apart,
Bob found both time to help me and open his heart.
Against all odds we became close friends,
So I dedicate this poem and the message it sends.

Bob was a constant reminder that "somebody cared,"
And I'll forever cherish the visits we shared.
My friend passed away a short time ago,
But I believe our bond in the Lord still can grow.

May you rest in peace, Bob, my dear old friend,
And receive all the love that I'm trying to send,
Across the miles and all through the years.
Thanks for sharing my smiles; thanks for easing my fears.

"Many receive advice, only the wise profit from it."
                                        —*Publilius Syrus*

Yoga-Man

Soren Gordhamer

*F*or the third consecutive week, I stride into the youth division at Rikers Island in New York City to teach. Covered with massive fences and acres of barbed wire, this daunting correctional facility sits on an island in the East River. Housing roughly 16,000 inmates, Rikers meets the criteria as one of the largest city jails in the United States. Included in this total are roughly two thousand teens between the ages of 16 and 18, qualifying it as the largest youth jail in our country.

In order for me to get from the front gate to the classroom where I work with these teens, I must first pass through five checkpoints, a bridge, and six locked metal doors—a trip which takes about 45 minutes. The youth living here have done everything (or nothing) from truancy to murder.

I offer my classes as part of their school curriculum during the day. My first class is especially difficult. It's a large class of about 25 adolescents—most are interested, but those who aren't refuse to be quiet. The teacher is gone, so it's just me and the guys. I struggle to do my best, but I can't gain control of the group. I sit down and have a discussion with three kids who seem to be more engaged. I expect the teacher to come back, but he never does.

Relieved when my first class is finally over, I hurry to the next one where the teacher is present. As I take a deep breath to begin, a sizable young man comes barreling through the door. Banging on his chest, he announces, "The king is here!" He proceeds to give a two-minute monologue that I can't quite follow, but the gist of it seems to be a repeated assertion of his self-appointed leadership.

Then he walks over to me and shouts, "Who you?" Looking up at his massive features, I tell him my name. He lets me know that he goes by Mike. "What'cha doing in my class?" he asks.

I give him the short version of my usual rap. He shows mild interest. I get Mike and the ten others to pull their chairs into a circle. I begin by talking about how a variety of people use meditation and that even professional basketball teams like the Lakers meditate to help them get "in the zone" or "in the flow" during games. "What's it like to be in-the-zone?" I ask.

Mike responds, "You do what you need to do without worrying about it." I invite him to say more. "It's like when I was selling lots of drugs and making mad money—if I ever got afraid during a deal or if I wasn't paying attention, it would go bad. If I were confident, then it always worked out. I never worried, so it always worked out."

Through experience, I know that many young people like Mike can use the power of the mind in nefarious situations, but they're rarely shown how it can be used in positive, more constructive ways. Following up on one of Mike's comments, I add, "But it didn't always work out because . . . here you are."

Smiling, Mike responds, "Not for selling drugs. No one caught me for that!"

"So, what did you get caught for?" I ask, well aware that I'm heading into uncharted waters.

Leaning back in his chair, Mike cocks his head and stares at me for a moment. "Body," he responds. *Does he mean he committed murder?* I wonder. *If this were true, he wouldn't be in this unit, so I know he's only saying this to reinforce his "tough guy" image for the benefit of the class.*

I decide to shift gears and go back to our earlier discussion. "So how *did* you feel when you were doing a deal, Mike?"

"I felt like I had to be *on*—like I was alive."

"Part of the excitement for you was the fact that you had to be alert and watchful during a deal," I say. "We're all looking for the feeling of being fully alive. But some people only know how to achieve this feeling through dangerous activities. With danger we must be attentive. But maybe there is another way to experience this attentiveness. Today we will explore other ways to get to that place." Mike sits straight up in his chair. He appears to be hanging on my every word.

Then I guide the group through a short meditation. Things are going well. Everyone is focused. A few of them open their eyes briefly to see if Mike is participating too—closing them again after seeing him sitting quietly, eyes shut, like them. After I ring the Tibetan bells to end the meditation, a number of the kids smile in approval.

Next we discuss their life at the facility. After class, they will return to their regular routine on the unit, where they will have one hour of recreation time—and after that, nothing in particular. They'll probably play cards or watch television.

Knowing they have so much free time, I ask, "Why aren't there any programs like this in the evenings?" Mike, who seems to be their spokesperson, responds, "People are too scared. How many people want to come out at night to a unit of 50 convicted guys?"

Good point. I also know that another reason is a lack of funding for worthwhile programs. We pay 20 to 30 grand per year to keep each kid in prison. These kids will soon be back on the streets. How sad that cities across the country provide little or no funding for programs to help these youngsters make a positive change.

In the hallway, enroute to my next class, someone shouts, "Yoga-man!" I look up to see a familiar face. It's Chris waving me down. He was in my class a few weeks ago. Winded from running after me, he stops a moment to catch his breath. "Why didn't you come to my class today, Yoga-man?"

"I only go where they tell me I can go."

"Hurry up," Chris says, motioning for me to follow. "Come this way to my class, just for a few minutes." As we walk, he asks, "You got the bells with you?" I nod, feeling as if we're sneaking off to the bathroom to smoke a joint.

Following him into a room of eight kids, and no teacher, he gathers them up. "Yo! Check this out. We're going to do a meditation. Everybody chill and listen to him." I'm nervous, perspiring, afraid the teacher will show up. I tell them to close their eyes for the meditation. Chris breaks in, "Wait! They got a sit up straight first!" He models the posture. I tell them to sit up. We do a short meditation and end just as the teacher enters. She's grinning—probably shocked to see her class sitting in a circle looking tranquil.

Although I go into Rikers to teach meditation and yoga, I know that what matters most is the spirit of the work. I have to develop trust first.

Last week's yoga class proved to be quite challenging. I know a certain degree of posturing must occur before trust develops, but the kids were tense and guarded. During the class, a muscular guy, with the body of a street fighter and the face of a Taoist sage, asks, "Yoga-man, can this stretch help me get bigger muscles?"

With a serious expression, I look at him and answer, "Actually, if you do this enough, you can get really big muscles like me." As he scans my scrawny frame, I can almost hear him thinking. *Does this homie really think he has big muscles?*

Unable to keep a straight face, I let out a belly laugh. Within seconds, contagious laughter ripples throughout the classroom. What matters most is the spirit of the work.

"Silence is the great teacher, and to learn its lessons you must pay attention to it. There is no substitute for the creative inspiration, knowledge, and stability that come from knowing how to contact your core of inner silence."

—Deepak Chopra

A Sign from God

Jane Katenkamp

*F*or some strange reason I felt uncomfortable about our upcoming prison visit. I was puzzled. Jack and I had conducted Marriage Encounter programs at the same facility several times before. *Was I being silly?*

Leading these enrichment sessions for married inmates and their spouses always gave my husband and me the feeling that we were doing God's will. They filled us both with a sense of peace. *So, why was I apprehensive?*

Praying and reflecting on this dilemma, I finally pinpointed the source of my anxiety. It wasn't because I was afraid of going into the prison, after all. In truth, I was worried about spending so much time away from our five children.

Our daughter and four sons were good kids. Even so, I felt concerned and guilty. From the youngest, only eleven, to our oldest, nineteen—they were young and impressionable.

Through our volunteer experience with prison Marriage Encounter programs, Jack and I spent hours working with inmates and their spouses. We learned firsthand just how easily some kids, even good ones, can get into serious trouble. Although our prayer life was strong, Jack and I were still haunted by feelings of guilt for the time we spent away from our children—especially because of what had happened a few months earlier.

Close friends consented to having our children stay with them for the weekend while we conducted a program. Our son Jerry said, "Don't worry about me. I'll be staying with Brian." We knew Brian pretty well. He hung around our house often, so that decision seemed sensible.

Later we discovered that Brian had told his mom he would be spending the weekend at *our* house. It came as a shock when we found out these two thirteen-year-olds tried to sleep in the woods that night. A neighbor spotted them as they climbed onto our carport roof to sleep—around 2 a.m. I felt like a negligent mother.

After a long talk with his father and me, Jerry confessed, "I didn't have much fun. I barely slept anyway. I promise . . . I'll never do it again!"

Jerry was adventuresome. I was more concerned about leaving him than I was about leaving any of our other children. Praying for comfort, I begged God to give me a sign. I needed to know that Jack and I were doing the right thing—that our children wouldn't be adversely affected by the time we gave to others.

The next day, Jerry asked, "Mom, can I talk to you alone?" The two of us sat on the living room sofa, face to face. "Mom, do you remember Mark?" My mind raced to recall. "He's the new boy at school. His dad left home, and his mom didn't want him any more."

Suddenly the answer clicked. "Yes, I do. He just moved in with his aunt and uncle."

"That's right. We have this game at school. You go up to a boy, put up your fists and say, 'Ya wanna fight?' Then the other boy puts up his fists and says, 'Ya.' Next you say, 'Then join the army,' and walk away."

"Are they still playing that silly game? They played that when I was young," I chuckled.

Wearing a serious expression, Jerry moved closer to me. "Mom, I heard Mark go up to a boy today. He said, 'Ya wanna fight?' The other boy put up his fists and said, 'Ya!' but Mark said, 'Then get married!'"

Studying my stunned look with serious eyes, Jerry continued. "Mom, I'm really glad that you and Dad are doing that Marriage Encounter thing. If you help just one couple to stay together, like you and Dad, you'd be helping their kids too."

Tears filled my eyes. "Thank you for sharing that, Honey." We hugged, concluding our private conversation. Suddenly, I saw the beginnings of a man in the boy I'd worried so much about. I felt overjoyed because I knew my prayers had just been answered.

[EDITOR'S NOTE: For information on National Marriage Encounter Prison Ministry, Inc., contact 4704 Jamerson Place, Orlando, FL 32807; visit their Web site: http://www.marriage-encounter.org; or write to e-mail: NatlME@aol.com.]

"Listen to your children. They are prophets."

—Fr. Gabriel Calvo
Founder of Marriage Encounter

Conversion on the Job

Eric F. Bauman

What most Americans know, or think they know, about this country's penal system is largely based on imaginative paperback novels and sensationalized Hollywood film accounts.

My own knowledge is firsthand. For fifteen years, a substantial part of my life, I've worked as an officer in one of the nation's largest county correctional centers: a caretaker for society's outcasts, rebels, and predators. The ride has been bumpy emotionally, intellectually, and—surprise—spiritually.

Work in a correctional center as a corrections officer is not the ideal setting for a religious conversion. The socialization process leads elsewhere. My initial experience came at an impressionable moment in my life. I was twenty-four years old when I was given a badge and a uniform and, along with them—what I failed to see then—tremendous power over other human beings in a controlled environment. Not so much by direct instruction as by a sort of absorption, I learned and adopted the Us-versus-Them approach of my peers in uniform. I yearned to be accepted and trusted by them and struggled with the stigma of being a rookie.

And, of course, I brought with me into the job a full share of ignorance and bias. I recall my first experience with inmates as they lounged around inside a recreation room, watched television, and smoked cigarettes. I felt an immediate tension. Most of them were young black males; they seemed to stare right through me as I patrolled the area. Why would they do that? The only things that registered with me were the color of their skin and the rage they seemed to exhibit so freely. I passed instant judgment: These men—all of them—were morally depraved, and my natural enemies. I gave little if any consideration to life histories, family backgrounds, economic status, education, chemical dependency. These were not persons but inmates.

And I had control over them. I could reward or punish inmates for whatever reason I deemed fit. I could provide them with extra portions of food for conforming to the rules or punish any who showed contempt for me by cutting their contact visits short. Depending on my mood for the day, I could allow additional television time or curtail time on the telephone.

Moreover, I could use force. Violence can erupt at any moment inside a prison; guards are authorized to respond in kind, theoretically according to rules but actually at their own discretion. At first, I was uncomfortable using physical force in the line of duty, but with each incident it became easier. Finally, force became a routine way of dealing with inmate disturbances, whether or not it was justified. I earned a reputation among both inmates and fellow officers as one not to be messed with. After some time it became obvious that I would not hesitate to use force in any given situation, and I began to rely on this notoriety more and more. I could administer either verbal or physical discipline whenever I felt it was necessary, at my own discretion. Any thought of counterattack by the inmates died quickly; they were aware of the presence of "back-up" officers and of the severe penalties an inmate would incur for attacking an officer.

Over time, as I now realize, my outward behavior began to affect my inner self. After several years on the job, I found myself becoming abrupt and harsh with all those around me, analyzing situations cynically, cutting people apart with sarcasm—a frequent phenomenon among those charged with law enforcement. My only friends were those fellow officers whom I trusted. Because of my dark moods and sharpness, even my parents became distant from me. Perhaps because of this distance, I also began to be aware of my loneliness, a distinct sense of isolation that was totally unfamiliar to me. It was a solitary feeling, I now realize, but at the time it was hard to bear.

I recall feeling just this way, but in spades, one afternoon while riding alone on a prison elevator. I was on the verge of tears when the elevator stopped to pick up someone. As the door opened, I tried to hide my face in shame from the correction captain who entered. Knowing my reputation and sensing my embarrassment, she said nothing; but when the elevator stopped at her floor, she made one simple gesture that began the transformation that has led me to write this account. Without saying a word, she pulled from her pocket a small gold crucifix and gently placed it in the palm of my hand. I remember wanting to run, to escape from that place. I went to an isolated area where I could be alone and sat staring down at this figure, sobbing uncontrollably.

A second grace came to me around this time. Though I had been raised in a faithful Catholic family, I had long ago chosen to distance myself from the church and a God I viewed as absent rather than present. But when I encountered a friend from the old neighborhood, we exchanged confidences about feelings of loneliness we were both experiencing. He, his wife, and I decided to attend a weekend evening Mass together in the church from which we both had strayed. Because of the time I had been away and the guilt that seemed to consume me, the experience was uncomfortable. But I found relief that evening in the celebrant's homily on reconciliation and, eventually, in the encounter with those in the church community whom I came to know.

Thus began a process. In leisure time, I began to read about the church and about its past and present-day saints. A friendly parish priest encouraged me to continue attending Mass and to consider returning to school. He introduced me to others with similar experiences in their lives and jobs. At work, I began to set a distance between myself and those fellow workers I had once emulated and trusted. In small steps, I began to offer the inmates in my charge the same pardon and reconciliation I was receiving from the church.

These were positive steps, and yet the time was difficult and puzzling. Internally, I constantly questioned this need to become something different. My doubts were reinforced by my estrangement from other officers, some of whom ridiculed my new attitudes toward inmates and portrayed me as someone not to be trusted. Fortunately, or providentially, I was introduced to a sympathetic priest who offered encouragement and helped me to understand that anyone who decides to follow Christ in a serious way will encounter harassment from those made uncomfortable by that commitment.

His advice helped through the years that followed. I acted on the advice I had been given by completing my undergraduate degree in human services and continuing on to become a credentialed alcoholism counselor. I was now steering inmates into drug and alcohol programs inside the jail, scheduling appointments for them with vocational counselors, listening to them tell about their past lives. I've also counseled fellow officers afflicted with the disease of chemical dependency and with job-related problems. But to this day, six years later, I am still being confronted by skeptical/cynical peers who have nothing but scorn for my newfound attitudes toward the poor, the diseased, and the imprisoned.

Though their ridicule is still not easy to take, my academic studies have grounded me and given me confidence in the possibility of reaching those I am responsible for. My family has stood in support of me, and I am indebted to them for their understanding. My wife and I attend Mass together with our newborn son, Eric Joseph, sometimes on a daily basis. I now have a genuine sense of mission with regard to my life as a correction officer, so that this job I once loathed I now see as a blessing and a grace. As anyone who has followed this story can see, others have been occasions of grace for me, so that it does not seem presumptuous that I can hope by my behavior to teach something about human dignity and the meaning of the gospel.

It has not been easy for me to confront my own prejudices and weaknesses while at the same time questioning established and comfortable ways of dealing with the stresses of this work. But, from the story of the prodigal son to the dialogue between Christ and the thief on Calvary, I believe all people are constantly being called to conversion and challenged by that call. The biblical account I find most relevant to my own calling tells of Jesus' sharing a meal with people thought to be unworthy. Seeing this, the Pharisees asked his disciples why he would associate with such people. Jesus overheard them and replied, "People who are well do not need a doctor, but only those who are sick . . . I come to call not respectable people, but outcasts." By that standard, I'm in the right place at the right time, and I'm grateful.

6

Stumbling Blocks to Stepping Stones

"If we study the lives of great men and women carefully and unemotionally we find that, invariably, greatness was developed, tested and revealed through the darker periods of their lives. One of the largest tributaries of the river of greatness is always the stream of adversity."

—Cavett Robert

A Mother Again

Thomas Ann Hines

My only child was murdered. After twenty-one years I had spent loving and caring for Paul, a single bullet ripped through his heart and killed him. My life was shattered.

Paul attended college in Austin, 200 miles from our home in Plano, Texas. He was a good student, dated a lovely girl and did well in school. On Sunday evening we talked for an hour. Since I had a cold, he pressed me, "Why don't I come home and take care of my 'little mother'?"

"I'll be fine, Dear," I assured him. "Besides, I'm sure you have plenty of studying to do." I knew he had a test on Monday and needed to stay at school. Then we ended our conversation as we always did. "I love you, Mom. Take care of yourself."

With my usual motherly concern, I replied, "I love you, Paul. Please be careful."

"Don't worry, Mom," he replied. I heard Paul's voice for the last time.

The next night, February 18, 1985, a chilly Monday in Austin, Paul stopped to play games at an arcade. He planned to wait for Mandy, his beloved fiancée, while she finished studying for a test. Paul had promised to pick her up at 10:30. He had no inkling of what cruel fate awaited him.

Charles, a troubled seventeen year-old with several felonies on his record, was making plans. His attorney had made it clear that if Charles didn't leave town, he would find himself behind bars. Heeding the warning, Charles decided to steal a car and vanish, thereby escaping punishment for his offenses.

Charles observed Paul walking into the arcade, noted that he was alone and approached him with the pretense of needing help. Later, in a face-to-face meeting with Charles, in June of 1998, he told me what he had said to Paul. Charles pleaded, "My mother is sick on the other side of town. I think she might be dying. Would you give me a ride to her house? Please? I'm worried sick!" Charles was a good looking-young man, with a pleasant smile and winning personality. I could see why Paul agreed to give him a ride.

"Sure, Man. I understand about mothers," Paul replied. "I'll be glad to help you out." They both got into Paul's car and drove around as Charles gave directions for a while. When Paul pressed the teenager, "Hey, Man, what's your address?" Charles told him to pull into the parking lot of an apartment complex in the Riverside District, where many of the college students lived.

Paul did what he was told. When the car stopped, Charles ordered Paul to get out. Paul refused. Charles, aware that Paul would be able to identify him, panicked and pulled the trigger of the loaded pistol hidden in his pocket. One shot through Paul's heart and lungs, and he was dead.

As the days, weeks, months and years passed, I wrestled with the appropriate way to answer the recurrent question, "Do you have any children?" Rehearsing my response, I wondered, *Should I say, "I don't have any children?"* No, that would mean that Paul never existed. He was still very much alive in my heart and in my mind.

The first time I was confronted with this situation, I burst into tears and fled the room. People knew something was terribly wrong, but I wasn't able to talk about Paul's murder or explain that I was no longer a mother. I felt cheated. Then I read a pamphlet from The Compassionate Friends. I began to reply to the question by saying, "I *had* one son who was murdered in 1985."

People either responded by asking, "Do you want to talk about *it?"* or by apologizing for asking the question in the first place.

After being invited to participate in the first "behind the walls" prison Victim Impact Panel in 1994, I diligently prepared my presentation. On my ruled tablet, I listed all the thoughts that were in my aching heart. I fervently planned to tell the inmates just how horrible they were. I would tell *them* just what they had done to Paul; what they had done to Mandy; and what they had done to me and my family. And, I would tell them that, because of *them,* I would never again be a mother. I would never have grandchildren. I wanted *them* to know exactly how I felt.

I studied the assembled men—all 200 of them, clad in ghostly prison whites. As I listened to the first two speakers, I was shocked to see tears in some of their eyes. I thought, *They're really listening, and they actually have feelings!* Clutching my notes with steely resolve, my mind was riveted on how I was going to give *them* my message.

The speaker who preceded me, a lofty gentleman well over six feet, commanded a great deal more attention than my petite five-foot, three-inch frame. When the time came to deliver my message, I sauntered to the microphone.

I was in no hurry. After all, I wanted *them* to quiet down first and pay full attention to what I was about to say.

Approaching the microphone, I examined the crowd. I looked to my right, straight ahead and then to my left. My heart almost stopped as my eyes focused on a haunting face in the third row. I was struck by the cruel irony of this young man's red hair—the same shade as Paul's—and sky-blue eyes with glasses similar to the ones that Paul wore. And his slender build bore an eerie resemblance to Paul. They could have been brothers.

This young man's "hungry" eyes sought mine with an intense look that reached into my heart and soul. My mind raced. *He looks like a nice kid. How did he end up in prison?* As these troubled thoughts tumbled around in my heart, I thought, *What if this were my son? What would I want another mother to say to him?* It was as if the frost instantly melted away from my icy heart. For the first time in nine years, I felt like a mother again. A magnificent feeling of comfort came over me. Tossing my notes aside, I spoke from my heart—the true heart of a mother.

That day, so many years ago, I received a precious gift—one that only a child can give to a parent. I'm grateful to that redheaded boy for being there that day. When he opened his heart to me, I was finally able to open mine. And years later, I was able to open my heart to my son's murderer.

Every time I go into a prison as a volunteer to give a motivational talk to inmates, I receive countless gifts and inspiration from *their* words. Hearts continue to open inside prison walls.

[EDITOR'S NOTE: For information on The Compassionate Friends, Inc., contact Web site: http://www.compassionatefriends.org or write to P. O. Box 3696, Oak Brook, IL 60522-3696.]

Free Willie

Mary Rachelski

Whatever this seventeen-year-old did to get himself into prison, he must have backed in. Black and incredibly shy, his main flaw appears to be a lack of self-confidence. I doubt he has one prejudiced bone in his body.

Challenged by a characteristic lisp, Willie is soft spoken and has only good things to say about the people he comes into contact with—most likely the reason he ended up in a high-medium security prison. Trusting and willing to do anything for anyone, my guess is he trusted the wrong person. It takes Willie a little longer to "get it" (whatever "it" is), but when he does, he's as smart as the best of them. We just have to know how to put "it" into Willie's language. He aspires to be a zoologist when he grows up and reads everything he can about animals.

My maternal side wants to hold and rock him—to protect him from the darker side of prison life. I'd be content to do this until the guards open the gates and tell Willie he can go home to his mother where he belongs.

Picking up on vibes that he had done something to displease an older and wiser inmate, one that he and most of the other men looked up to as a mentor, Willie wore an expression comparable to a puppy who had just had his nose whipped by a rolled-up newspaper. No matter how hard I tried, Willie wouldn't allow me to intervene. He just kept saying, "Thank you Ms. Mary. I'll be fine." Now I've always had a problem with "bullies." I wanted to take this wise-mouthed, father-figure and pinch his ear lobe until he apologized to Willie. Instead, I chose to accept the fact that Willie was doing his best to grow up at his own pace.

One day, during our class, Willie finally got his "day in the sun." This session, designed to show the inmates how to locate and remove roadblocks from their lives, afforded them the opportunity to discover their own potential. I had the men reading common phrases that can prevent a person from moving out of the detrimental cycle of negative thinking. Since this tends to be a boring activity for kinesthetic learners (those who learn best by doing—being involved) we try to make the exercises as action-packed as possible.

To demonstrate how harebrained their excuses sometimes sound when perceived in the right setting, I conducted a "read off." During this friendly competition the men tried to "outdo" each other while attempting to show emotion in their voices. My husband facilitates these classes with me. Willie approached my husband and said, "This sounds like poetry to me. I'd like to read it to the class." Up until now Willie had never read aloud, so naturally, we assumed his reading skills were limited— not uncommon in prison.

When an inmate wants to break a barrier in our class we usually let him, provided he doesn't infringe on anyone else's rights. As Willie began to read, we stood there with our mouths hanging open. "I can't get a loan, I've got a record. People don't give jobs to ex-cons. Can't get no breaks. Life's a bummer." Never in our three-plus years of presenting this program had anyone done a more eloquent and moving reading. The thunderous applause, cheers, and whistles bounced off the walls. Everyone was moved, but none was so moved as Willie. He had discovered a gift.

Today he is still in prison. He is a cameraman for the Jaycees. On Thursdays and most Fridays he talks to kids. Willie is now part of an elite alliance of inmates who go through rigorous training and keep a strict code of ethics to be allowed to be a Youth Awareness Group member. Each week, thirty at-risk kids are brought into the prison by their counselors or parole officers to spend time with Willie and twenty other inmates who tell these youngsters, in no uncertain terms, just what's in store for them if they choose to continue living their current lifestyles.

[EDITOR'S NOTE: For more information on the Jaycees, contact P.O. Box 7, Tulsa, OK 74102-0007; Web site: http://www.usjaycees.org.]

"Stand up to your obstacles and do something about them. You will find that they haven't half the strength you think they have."

—*Norman Vincent Peale*

Death Row Overflow

Mike Chernock

My friends all think of my pal, Roland, and me as really good people. But they only see two helpers bringing weekly church services, Eucharist, and baptism into the AIDS ward at San Quentin Hospital. They don't know we went kicking and screaming into this ministry, just as we did with all the other volunteer activities we participate in.

A cardinal rule of volunteering in prison is never to ask or tell the nature of a person's crime. Aside from privacy issues, telling distorts the relationship so much that it challenges the volunteer to see the resident on equal terms. That's probably why this incident sticks out so vividly in our minds.

It was not unusual for the chaplain to ask us to visit a particular resident for any number of reasons, but during this assignment he slipped and told us the offense was child molestation. At the time, my own daughters were in grade school.

The chaplain went on to say that this twenty-one-year-old, brought in less than three days before, had been placed in administrative protective-isolation after several severe beatings by other inmates. The beatings had left his glasses broken, his face battered almost beyond recognition, and his psyche in a state of confusion and extreme withdrawal.

The resident's cell number was unfamiliar, and the search led us into a completely foreign area of the prison. On the wall, next to the huge oak and steel door, were two ominous looking signs. The first read: NOTICE! WARNING SHOTS WILL NOT BE FIRED IN THIS AREA. And the second stated: OFFICERS AND VISITORS MUST WEAR FLAK JACKETS AT ALL TIMES BEYOND THIS POINT.

As we read the signs, we knew that we were in the wrong place. God's call to prison ministry surely didn't mean for us to be here. The unexplainable appearance of an immense, in-our-face officer halted our hasty departure. To our chagrin, instead of ushering us out, he validated our credentials and assured us we were in the correct place.

It took a strong person to open the steel-framed, solid oak, gold-rush-era door. We cautiously entered the redbrick, earthquake-reinforced building, squinting until we adjusted to the darkness. We found ourselves in the first of three sets of cages, each with its own guard and locked security doors. Although the other officers seemed surprised by our presence, the one who accompanied us verified that our credentials were in order.

Hoping to be turned away at each gate, we found ourselves passing through, one after the other. In the third cage, a stern middle-aged matron snapped, "Where are your flak jackets?"

Her odd question evoked my involuntary, smart aleck retort, "Well, you know how it is with those darn jackets . . . always leaving them in the other car."

She smiled and said, "I know what you mean. I do it all the time." As she opened the final cage door, we realized our brave "snappy patter" had dashed our last hope for escape.

Behind the last door, we found a special kind of "hell." Five tiers of cells, each holding a single inhabitant, one bunk, a dim light, and an open toilet secured to the floor. The bars had been welded over with steel mesh to prohibit the passage of even a small pencil. Besides the customary locks, each door had an additional padlock about the size of the back of a man's hand. The only opening to the cell was a single slot barely large enough to pass through a sheet of paper. Crude insults bombarded us from faceless, shadowy figures in adjoining cells.

Eventually we found our young man's cell. Only semi-coherent, he spoke in scarcely intelligible, disjointed phrases. "Could someone bring me a Bible? . . . How's my mom? . . . Could you tell me how to get my glasses fixed?"

Although most volunteers want desperately to make a difference and say the right things at the right time, sometimes prison ministry consists of nothing more than merely sitting in mutual silence and departing with a simple prayer—precisely what we did that day. Even the trip home lacked its usual repartee.

The following week, Roland went alone. On his way to the hospital, he stopped to re-visit the same young man. Roland was tersely informed that a visit was utterly impossible. The cell in question was in the overflow area for death-row inmates and off limits to all but a handful of permanent staff. When the volunteer attempted to assure the officers that we had already been there the previous week, assurances came forth, "That incident absolutely could not have happened."

Half a year later, daily routines and other memorable incidents caused the event to fade in our minds. We almost began to think perhaps it never happened—until the day

---

I walked into the prison hospital alone. Suddenly, I found my arms bound to my sides by a resident who appeared out of nowhere. Since the rules forbid an embrace in our prison, this was a harrowing experience. I attempted to free myself and grab my emergency whistle. Then I saw the tears and recognized the familiar young face—the face of the young man we had met months before in death row overflow.

I managed to mumble something inappropriate, "Do you know the whole story about our visit that day?" He released me. When I was able to focus, I found myself looking into the biggest tear-stained grin I'd ever seen.

"Oh yeah . . . ain't God great?" he said, and then he disappeared into a sea of denim pants and shirts.

"Nothing splendid has ever been achieved except by those who dared believe that something inside them was superior to circumstance."

—Bruce Barton

"Hey, I ordered mine supersized with onion rings!"

Reprinted by permission of Tom Prisk.

"It is not the size of a man but the size of his heart that matters."

—*Evander Holyfield*

Hungry for Freedom

Shannon Grillo

*T*he powdery snowfall silently coated the uninviting prison yard with tranquil white layers that glistened in the glow of the floodlights.

Assigned to the task of removing snow from the sidewalks, a correctional officer accompanied Christie and me outside. We went right to work, hiding our glee, trying not to enjoy our task quite so much. Now, this might seem like an ordinary occurrence, but that frigid December night was different—at least for me.

We were rarely allowed out at night, especially on one so peaceful. I found myself caught up in overwhelming feelings of nostalgia. Wonderful childhood memories of snowmen, Christmas and, of course, my long-lost freedom. I endured the strenuous labor of shoveling a sidewalk the size of two city blocks in order to dwell within my own thoughts. The recollections were sweet but accompanied by a hunger to be free, despite the fact I still had years remaining on my sentence.

Christie and I took our time shoveling—making the normal twenty-minute chore into one that took more than twice as long. After we finished, we hesitated for just a second to take in the crisp, serene night air before returning to the madness of prison life.

As I peeled off my damp clothes, a voice over the intercom told me to report to the Lieutenant's office. Exhausted, I trudged across the dayroom and entered the office.

The Lieutenant said, "You did such a great job, I want you to shovel the walkway in front of the building." Realizing this meant more peace and quiet time, I eagerly responded, "Okay." Climbing back into my soggy clothes, I marched outside with my shovel and an officer.

By then, it was around 9:30. The increasingly heavy snowfall had sculpted a picturesque landscape. Visibility from the watchtower was poor, and the front of the building was outside the confines of the prison fence. I stood in the parking lot, looking out at the iridescent night, and tasted freedom. All at once, those memories came flooding back to me. Like a blinding blizzard, conflicting thoughts clouded my mind. *I could become the savage the jury found me guilty to be. With one last act of violence, I could leave now and savor freedom, even if for a moment.*

Tightening my grip on the shovel, I stood behind the officer and entertained thoughts of violence. I told myself, *All it would take is one swift swing, and I could knock him unconscious.*

"My side of the walkway is done, Sir," I announced. "I'm ready to go in."

While I waited for the officer to open the gate, I remembered. *The last time I stood here, I was wearing shackles and handcuffs. Now I'm standing here, of my own free will, with freedom screaming behind my back.* That was the moment when I realized I must face all the skeletons in my closet if I truly wished to be free.

After going inside, I cried in the only private place around—the shower. There, I released those overwhelming thoughts of madness. That snowstorm helped me make a choice, the right one—to face what lies ahead. That night was different. It opened up a whole new side of me—one that would allow my soul to heal.

"In the last analysis, our only freedom is the freedom to discipline ourselves."

—*Bernard M. Baruch*

Giving Birth to Joy

Kim Book

*D*ear Nicole,

How I wish you could be here. I have so many things I want to share with you. But I know that you are in a much better place and that someday we will be together again—for eternity.

I was thinking about you today and how your death has profoundly changed my life. It's hard to explain the peace and joy that I have in my heart because of you. Nearly six years ago, we looked into one another's eyes and said, "I love you." Today, I can no longer look into your loving eyes, but you will remain in my heart always.

On the day you were murdered, I thought I could never go on. After all, Nicole, you were my only child, my beautiful daughter and we had so much left to do. Suddenly our future was shattered. But this letter is not about what I have lost; it is about what I have found.

The first year after your death, I felt as if I were walking around in a fog. After I realized I had forgiven the young man who murdered you, my life began to change. I felt as if a weight had been lifted from my shoulders. I felt free. My heart no longer felt heavy, and I thanked God for allowing me to forgive. I wanted to share with others the peace I have felt from this act of forgiving, so they might come to understand how something positive could come from something so tragic.

Today, Nicole, my life is full, and the past five years have been joyous. Four years ago, I began volunteering in the prison system. I conduct Bible studies and other programs that help men and women understand what it means to be the victim of a crime.

Many inmates have told me that they see God in me, and nothing humbles me more than that statement. I have worked with people who have committed murders, people much like the young man who took your life. They, too, want to be forgiven. When I tell them, "God has forgiven you," I see joy in their eyes.

Every year at Christmas, our church participates in the Angel Tree program where we adopt children of incarcerated parents and buy gifts for them. We always have a wrapping-party at our house. You would like that, Nicole. You loved to wrap gifts.

Being able to help the inmates give gifts to their children at Christmas brings me much satisfaction. When I look at all those gifts sitting around the house, I can almost feel your presence right beside me.

I wish I could tell you about the wonderful friends I have made because of your death and how they have become like family to me. The fragile fifteen-year-old girl in the detention center who lost her twins when she was only thirteen and asks me simply for a hug because she knows I care. The grieving mother whose son committed suicide tells me she admires my strength in God and the joy I have found. And the halfway house where I lend a helping hand. I feel blessed.

Losing you, Nicole, is the hardest reality I have ever had to face. You would be happy to know that my grief has given birth to the joy I feel today. I believe you are here with me in all that I do. Whenever I share my love with a prisoner, a homeless person, a young girl in a detention center, or even the young man who murdered you—I feel your presence. We're doing this together. You will never be gone.

I find joy in the things I do for others. I know that one day I'll hear the words, "Well done, good and faithful servant." And when I do, I know I'll look up and see your beautiful, smiling face once again—and we'll be reunited.

My love forever,
Mom

[EDITOR'S NOTE: Angel Tree is a part of Prison Fellowship Ministries. For additional information, contact Web site: http://www.prisonfellowship.org or see a prison chaplain.]

"Forgiveness is the eye of the needle. Unless you experience forgiveness you are never going to get your spirit back."

—*Caroline Myss, Ph.D.*

One Magical Hour

Diane Cook

*O*ne by one, they filed through the door and rounded the corner of the modest chapel, about the size of a college classroom. This orderly procession of drug dealers, thieves, and murderers seemed endless as they filled every available seat.

The soft hum of their voices tumbling off institutional tan walls drew my attention. Some carried Bibles, most carried nothing, but here they would find refreshing diversion in an unpleasant place.

I looked around to check on the rest of my team— ten amateur dramatists: seven women and three men committed to bringing live performances to people in confinement. This visit to the men's prison was the first of many to come.

Noticing that one of our actors was pale and trembling, I leaned toward her and whispered, "Are you all right?" She glanced at me briefly and offered a quick nod.

Despite my well-trained look of confidence, my mind's voice replied, *I'm glad* you *are.* Then an uneasy little voice inside me said, *I haven't a clue why we're here. What could we have been thinking?*

My eyes followed the men who were still processing in, from back to front. My heart almost stopped when I saw a young man slip into the front row. He leaned down, casually pulled the desktop up over his lap and started beating out "ratta-ratta-rat" with his right hand and "tat-tat" with his left. He tapped rhythmically to the ever-present beat that inhabits a drummer's mind. My son, about his age, did the same thing. *What could you have done to end up in this place?* my mind's voice questioned while my mother's heart broke for this young man.

Our one-hour program of sketches and songs seemed to pale in light of the harsh, dark realities that imprisoned these men. Nevertheless, they still came. Half an hour later, more than 200 men, young and old, filled the chapel.

"Tonight we have the CTM Players with us," announced an inmate who doubled as assistant chaplain. "Our choir will not be singing this evening because we don't want to miss any part of this special program."

Then it was time for the show to begin. The audience stirred in anticipation as I rose from my seat and walked to the microphone. My job, to start the program and keep it moving, was suddenly the farthest thing from my mind. The only move I wanted to make was right out the door.

Okay, Lord, I quietly prayed. *What now?* As I picked up the microphone a hush fell over the audience. I scanned their faces; and then, much to my own surprise, I began to mimic part of a sketch I had written three years earlier.

My staccato, twangy, mock-Southern style comment, "Phw, phw, phw!" followed by "Am I awnah?" (an exaggeration of "on") bounced off the walls like a ping-pong ball. I stared at the men in wide-eyed innocence. For almost a full second, silence gripped the room, as all eternity seemed to hold its breath. Then, laughter rolled through the chapel as the tension melted away.

Taped music led me into a song of hope, faith, and moving forward despite the circumstances. We were on a roll as we slipped into our first comedy sketch about two couples lunching together after Sunday church service. Our magical hour continued as we alternated between song and sketch, and back again.

When I sing, I always maintain eye contact with the audience—it helps drive the message home. During my second number, I was so focused on telling a story through song that I was unaware of the altercation unfolding in the front row. A subtle tension inched through the crowd as one of the officers escorted an inmate down the steps, behind me, and out the door. Totally oblivious, I continued my tale, not missing a beat. As the final notes faded away, the extra burst of enthusiastic applause took me by surprise.

Then it was time for the take-away—encouragement through music and mime to light our world. Our cast was nearly undone by the men's response to our sketch's character, the "frustrated brother," as he tried to "light his candle another way." The crowd called out, "Take it, Man, take it!" Genuine sounds of disappointment followed the actor's refusal. Moments later, when that same "frustrated brother" joined the family to form a beacon of light, the men were on their feet cheering.

As our troupe separated, the human beacon split and proceeded to light imaginary candles held by each man occupying an aisle seat. Once lit, each man passed the light to the one beside him and so on down the rows. I could almost see the flickering flames fan out across the room. As the inmates cheered, I felt embarrassed by my initial reluctance.

Then, like a puff of smoke, the magic vanished. Reality quickly set in as the officers began to escort the men from the chapel. Risking a momentary stop to shake our hands and thank us for coming, these inmates seemed like ordinary, everyday people trapped in an unholy fraternity.

Like the prisoners, we soon followed an officer from the chapel. Three steel gates crashed behind us as we retraced our steps to the parking lot. Like magic, we were changed from performers back into ordinary people with everyday lives—a homemaker, reporter, dental assistant, secretary, electrician, computer technician, teacher, and nurse.

"Courage and perseverance have a magical talisman, before which difficulties disappear and obstacles vanish into air."

—John Quincy Adams

Prison Brat

Cathy Roberts, CCM

You might call me a prison brat. My entire life has revolved around corrections. Indeed, most of my family, my husband's family, and I are career corrections employees. We live and work in a community with dangerous, desperate individuals, and our lives are on the line daily.

My memories of growing up in the prison community of Louisiana State Penitentiary, on 18,000 acres, are of happy childhood times. Building camps in the woods, playing "kick the can," riding bikes, skating at the recreation center, stealing a stalk of sugar cane from the field, and watching baseball games at the ball park were all part of my joyful existence at Angola. Isolated and sheltered as children, we were unaware of events that occurred within the prison.

Ours was the original "gated community." Crime in our neighborhood was virtually non-existent. Doors were seldom locked. Our unique society consisted of prison employees and their families; everyone knew everyone else and their business. We were as likely to be disciplined by our neighbor as by our own parents.

We were sandwiched into classrooms at a tiny elementary school six miles outside the prison gate. Most of the kids, whose parents were prison employees, now work at the prison themselves.

Most families rarely traveled to the nearest country town, 25 miles down a twisted winding road, until their children went to high school. We drove to Baton Rouge only twice a year—for back-to-school supplies and Christmas shopping. There was no real need to leave the grounds. Angola had its own commissary and U.S. Post Office. A prison doctor provided emergency medical care. I recall having stitches sewn by inmates on two occasions. When I showed up with a gash in my knee, I asked, "Could you please use pink thread?" Little wonder they chuckled.

Every morning prisoners delivered milk to our door, produced from the dairy herd. The "free store" for employee use contained fresh vegetables, grown and harvested from the lush plantation of Angola. Inmates also pumped our gas, cut our lawns, and cleaned some of the workers' houses.

In 1973, I graduated from high school and enrolled in a business college in Baton Rouge. It was difficult for my parents. They watched as their teenage daughter departed each morning for the 60-mile, one-way trip down that treacherous highway. But with prayer, a good breakfast, and a pistol cached under the seat of my car, off I went.

My mom worked in the nucleus of the prison—the Control Center. She was responsible for periodic inmate counts, radio traffic, the switchboard, and all alerts. Staffed with four employees on weekdays, her job was demanding. On weekends, only one officer worked each shift.

The year I attended business college, I spent most Sundays near the Control Center, where I could be near my mom and have my car washed by an inmate orderly. Several times I forgot to remove my pistol from the car before the inmate started washing it. The orderly always responded, "Miss Cathy, you need to come get your pistol."

My career in corrections began in 1974 at the Louisiana State Penitentiary. Since then I have seen many positive changes. Angola has earned worldwide acclaim as a progressive prison; violence has been reduced to the lowest numbers in decades. Our warden's philosophy: "The institution will treat you as well as you allow us to treat you." Opportunities and religious programs abound for those who wish to access them.

As a clerical staff member in prison administration, my exposure to inmates is limited to reading reports of violence. Now and then I wonder, *How could these be the same people? The ones I trusted and who were trustworthy enough to notify me that I had forgotten to remove my gun from my car? How could these men, who comforted a small girl getting stitches in her knee, commit such atrocities?* The answer—these prisoners are individuals, capable of violence, as well as kindness and caring.

Yes, you can call me a prison brat. Prison is my life. Angola has been my home for 43 of my 47 years. I love my life and my community. Who else could call a neighbor at 6 a.m. to rescue a lizard lodged in their kitchen sink?

Upon my retirement, I'll discharge my sentence. But unlike some inmates, my thoughts will not be focused on getting as far away from prison as possible. I'll be residing in that small country town, 25 miles outside the gate. My family, and the friends I've been blessed with during my employment, will keep me close to Angola.

7

Planting Seeds
of Wisdom

"A wise man never knows all. Only fools know everything."

—*African Proverb*

True Freedom

Linda Larsen

*H*e slowly lifts his gun and aims it directly between my eyes. He methodically cocks the trigger, closes one eye, as if for greater accuracy, and with a thin voice asks, "Are you ready to die?"

I am frozen. I am stunned. Wasn't it just a moment ago that I was sitting behind the receptionist's desk at work when this unknown man ran through the door? And yes, I do remember hearing him say as he dragged me across the street, "Don't call the cops or I will kill her!" I get the bizarre feeling that I am watching a surreal movie. Detached, yet absurdly involved.

Here I now sit, in the abandoned house where he plans to wait until dark. As I stare down the barrel of his .357 Magnum, I am acutely aware of the split. Two distinct people are in my head, jockeying for first position, for control over the ultimate outcome: a terrified woman and the Survivor.

The Survivor is calculating escape strategies at breakneck speed, analyzing every minute detail with superior precision. She has one intention—to get me out of this unbelievable nightmare alive. As odd as it seems, she has one obstacle even greater than the escaped convict with nothing to lose on the other end of the gun. She has to deal with the other me, the Panic-Stricken One, the one running around in circles, arms flailing wildly, screaming, crying and groveling for mercy. This one is completely out of control. The insane situation has total power over her and her sensibilities. The Survivor, on the other hand, is wielding her power over the situation. In the face of this craziness she has an enormous advantage. Her power is extremely channeled and focused with pinpoint accuracy on its target. She knows exactly what to do.

After a carefully calculated pause, the Survivor speaks, slowly and deliberately. "If you're going to kill me, I guess there's not much I can do to stop you."

I watch the words float out into space and hang in the air. The Panic-Stricken One is screaming inside my head, *What did you say that for, you idiot? Quick! Take it back! Take it back!*

The man continues to point his gun at me. Time is now suspended with a surreal echo in what seems like forever. Finally, he slowly lowers the gun. His eyes narrow slightly as his head cocks imperceptibly to the right.

"Why aren't you down on the floor begging and pleading for your life?" he asks.

The Survivor quickly scans her computer-brain for the correct response. Ah, there it is. She takes a purposeful breath, looks him directly in the eye and with the exact right mix of respect and confidence, she responds, "Because you are in control of this situation. If you want to kill me, you can. There's nothing I can do. You are in control. You have the power."

And for the first time since this horror began three hours earlier, the man looks confused.

In this moment I get it. I have the power. I am in control. I am the Survivor. In my mind I square off with the Panic-Stricken One and grab her by the shoulders. I tell her to relax, leave everything to me and trust. I assure her that I know what to do, and I will get us out alive.

And get us out is exactly what I ultimately did. At precisely the right instant, I made my escape through an unlocked door. It was the "make or break" moment, and I will say I wasn't quite sure which way it was going to go. At one point I could have sworn I heard gun shots behind me, but they simply turned out to be another grotesque fear making them sound and appear real. After a short distance, I was intercepted by the police and taken to safety. I learned later that, after he ran from the house we were in, he kidnapped a woman and her two children, forcing them to take him to another location. There he was finally apprehended.

Now, looking back on that dramatic event, I have a wider perspective. I see that the entire experience was a tremendous life lesson about power. In the days and weeks that followed, I not only began the process of dealing with the obvious trauma to my system, but I also began to see the experience as a metaphor for how to gain control and power in my life—no matter what the circumstances. I saw that two distinct parallels could be drawn between that event and other challenging situations in my life.

What I experienced of power as I was growing up was anything but positive. I was raised in a home with an alcoholic mother and a substantial amount of physical and mental abuse. By the age of twenty, I was married and divorced with a baby. I also began having severe, debilitating panic attacks around that time.

In fact, on the morning I was kidnapped, Pearl Harbor Day 1969, I awoke with the all-too-familiar, breath-stealing anxiety and found myself seriously considering suicide. I was filled with an oppressive sense of dread that made me feel that if I had to live my life like this—hanging onto my sanity by a flimsy string—I simply could not do it.

I wanted out. It wasn't the first time I'd had these feelings. But in spite of my emotions, I forced myself to go to work.

Isn't it ironic that four hours later an escaped convict would ask me if I was ready to die and offer me a one-way ticket out?

What I later began to realize is that my life, up until that time, had been a theme song for living in a state of powerlessness and despair. Certainly anyone who has lived with an alcoholic parent knows well the sense of helplessness which permeates his or her life. And the choices I continually made after I left home were ones subconsciously designed to keep me in that familiar state.

I believe (and this is merely an interpretation on my part) that my being kidnapped and held hostage for five hours was a huge gift to me. It was as if God were saying, "Okay, you think you want to die. I happen to know that you have amazing, wonderful things to accomplish in this life. I know that your life has the potential to be absolutely rich with joy and abundance and positive power. But if you can't see that right now, I guess I will have to resort to putting you in a situation where you will see it."

I'm not sure I could have gotten the message any other way.

I came to another extremely important realization through this experience. I was not this man's victim. I was my own victim—and had been for many years. He actually helped liberate me. How, therefore, could I possibly condemn him, especially since the terror I saw in his eyes merely reflected my own?

For years I had given my power away—to the highest bidder, to the strongest person, to the angriest aggressor. And in one auspicious, terrifying, amazing day—a desperate, escaped convict made it possible for me to get it back. I was truly set free.

The Complete Package

Diane Hamill Metzger

One of my ventures into volunteerism began when I was asked to participate in a program called Juvenile Pride and Awareness. In this program, various community programs for at-risk juveniles bring groups of their kids into the prison, where selected volunteer prisoners attempt to instill pride in them as individuals and to make them aware of where their current behavior can lead them. The program is often harsh but always tempered with love, and many times tears are shed on both sides as prisoners relate the tragedies of their own lives.

Early in my participation with this program, I was asked to speak one-on-one to a fourteen-year-old girl named Angela who had been placed into the program because of violent confrontations with her mother. She was also pregnant, angry and scared.

At first, Angela was reticent—not wanting to open up or to appear weak. So, respecting her silence, I began telling her the story of how I wound up in prison at twenty-five and why I was still here a quarter of a century later. I saw the interest and respect awaken in her eyes. She asked question after question, and pretty soon she began sharing some of her own experiences. We became so wrapped up in our conversation that two hours later her group searched us out and told us it was time for her to go.

Noting her dismay, I invited her to write to me, not really thinking she would. A couple of days later I was delighted to receive a letter from her at mail call. This simple connection between two human beings has resulted in a wonderful friendship and ongoing correspondence. I have pictures in my photo album of her baby boy, now a toddler, and I'm sometimes asked to mediate arguments that occasionally crop up between Angela and her mother.

Angela has returned to school and is doing well. She has great hopes for her future and tells me that I've played a large part in turning her life around. Whether it's a large part or any part, nothing can describe my satisfaction in watching a young life go the right way, especially after having my own take such a tragic detour.

Having been a volunteer inside of prison walls for many years, I can honestly say that my life would have been poorer had I not taken part. I will continue to volunteer for as long as I'm here, and I have no doubt that public service will continue to be a large part of my life once I'm free.

To me, the gift I can offer to others is only part of the package. The other part, the gift to me, is the contented feeling in my heart when I see what giving of myself can accomplish. It's the incredible realization that, no matter where I am and no matter what my circumstances, I'm still important because I can give to others.

The best way to find yourself is to lose yourself in the service of others."

—*Mahatma Gandhi*

"Looks like she's having a bad hair day."

Reprinted by permission of Christian Snyder.

"For to be free is not merely to cast off one's chains, but to live in a way that respects and enhances the freedom of others."

—*Nelson Mandela*

Another Word for Love

Jean Hull Herman

N ever before had I passed through clanging gates and grilled doors that closed behind and then opened ahead to guards and all those men.

Young men, old men, ageless men, lined-up, walking in file, guarded. They hadn't seen a girl in a long, long time, I deduced from the rustling and almost whistled whispering. Guarded lest they be identified and . . . and what? I didn't want to know.

By now, I was sure that this was a mistake: a woman, armed only with poetry, going to an inmate program, to talk to a select group of men who had beaten their addictions and were about to go free. *Those guards are still there, right? Just checking.*

I walked into a large unit—I think it's referred to as a POD—onto an open floor lined with lots of chairs. In those chairs sat a large group—more than 60 extremely courteous, quiet, attentive men in white jumpsuits—all staring at me. After a brief introduction, I was left standing there, up front, by myself . . . solo.

The men were expecting to be bored. Poetry—yawn! But they weren't. First, I read them some poetry, including rap lyrics, hip-hop, and some classical stuff (without calling it classical, so they would stay with me)—sticking to general topics. I talked about how writing serves to express feelings. By now, they no longer slouched down in their chairs, looking cool; they were sitting upright. We were talking to each other. They asked for poems on one topic or another.

When we came to questions and answers, the last question was: "I write my girlfriend and tell her I love her all the time, in every letter. I tell her over and over because I want her to wait for me. But is there some other way to say 'I love you?' Where do I find these other words?"

Remembering the small room I'd spotted earlier, with books and things in it, I asked, "Is there a thesaurus in your library?" An officer quickly found one and passed it along to me. With thesaurus in hand, I walked down the aisle to an older man who was standing behind the back row, showed him how to look up "love," and then turned to the pages where all the 'other words' were. I read about ten of them. When I looked up from the page, the man had tears in his eyes. Handing him the book, I walked back to the front of the room. I said my thanks, made my good-byes and left with my escort.

This poem comes from that experience.

Baby, I love you.
Baby, baby, I love you to death.
Honey, you know I love only you,
Want to be with just you and nobody else,
Want you to wait for me…

This makes one hundred times I've written the same thing.
Every day, I tell her, 'Baby, I love you.'
Now she says she wants to hear more than just that.
Though I live within iron and steel and uniforms,

Eat bad food and wear this prison gear,
I found out about a book of words called a thesaurus.
I always thought words were for other people,
For stupid school work, stuff I couldn't do,
So I didn't care about it.
Guys understand guys. We don't need no words.

But girls need words, I guess, so here goes:
My darling: I long to hug you, kiss you, caress your face,
Nuzzle and embrace you, enfold you in my loving arms.
Sweetheart, dearest one, you are my inamorata forever –
My own beloved.

I could get to like this.
Wonder what other magical books there are?

"The source of love is deep in us, and we can help others realize a lot of happiness. One word, one action, one thought can reduce another person's suffering and bring that person joy."

—Thich Nhat Hanh

My Convict Tutor

William J. Buchanan

I first saw "Swede" Garrison one March morning in 1937 when I was 11 years old. Flanked by guards, his arms handcuffed before him, he climbed the wide entrance steps to the Kentucky State Penitentiary at Eddyville where my father was warden. As I hurried past him toward a waiting school bus, our eyes met, and an uneasy expression crossed his face. Then, quickly, the icy mask returned. Curious, I watched until the mammoth steel gate clanged shut behind him. That was my first encounter with the man who would have a strange and lasting influence on my life.

Soon afterward, my father assigned the new inmate to work in central administration, near the warden's office. This led to an argument I heard about years later.

"It's a mistake, warden," the deputy warden insisted. "Garrison is big league, absolutely maximum security."

"I'm aware of Garrison's reputation, Porter," my father replied. "He's dangerous and he's brilliant. Not exactly a combination to put faith in. Yet, something about him intrigues me. I'm convinced that he's sincerely contrite. And I have strong feelings that a little trust right now just might bring out a positive side of his nature where strict

SERVING TIME, SERVING OTHERS

retribution wouldn't. No . . . the assignment stands. I want Swede Garrison at a useful job in the front office where I can see him every day."

In his late thirties, of average build, with bold, Nordic features topped by close-cropped blonde hair, Edwin S. Garrison was known to lawmen and the underworld alike as "Big Swede"—a tribute to his formidable reputation rather than to his size. In the early 1930s, following the repeal of prohibition, Swede graduated from whiskey smuggling along the Canadian border to big-time bookmaking in the lucrative tri-state gambling area around Cincinnati. The racket was tailor-made for his unique wizardry with figures. A mathematical genius, Swede could mentally calculate fluctuating racetrack odds ahead of the pari-mutuel machines and call them to the bookmaker before they were posted—a distinct house advantage.

As the casinos prospered, Swede became a well-known figure both in the underworld, and in country club circles. Although the target of frequent investigations, he skillfully outmaneuvered state and federal agents for years. Then, at the pinnacle of power and influence, he made the error that toppled him.

In that turbulent era, feuds between rival underworld gangs often erupted into open warfare. By the mid-1930s a gambling casino operated by a rival faction on the Kentucky side of the Ohio River was cutting deeply into Swede's take. Boldly, he decided to eliminate the competition by eliminating the rival casino. In the predawn hours one morning, Swede and his confederates broke into the basement of the casino and triggered several home-made firebombs. Unknown to Swede, three members of the night watchman's family were asleep on the premises. Two escaped, but a third person died in the fire. Swede testified that he was severely burned trying to rescue the victim. Although controversial, his testimony saved him from the electric chair. He was convicted by the Campbell

Circuit Court of Kentucky for "willful murder and arson" and sentenced to life imprisonment.

After school, I often did my homework in the prison administration office and talked freely with the convicts working there. Except for Swede. Entrenched in a corner behind a ledger-stacked desk, coldly impressive despite the office trusty's garb of starched khakis, he ignored me completely. As time passed without a word between us, I decided he neither knew nor cared that I existed. Until one Saturday.

I was doing homework on an adding machine and was barely aware of a heated religious argument between two inmate clerks.

"God!" one scoffed. He flourished a dollar bill. "This is the God the smart guy worships."

Suddenly, from the corner came the sounds of a ledger slamming shut and a chair pushed back in anger. Glancing up I saw the money-flourisher's face drain to a sickly pallor.

Swede was standing. His steel-blue eyes fiercely fixed on the hapless clerk. "Never forget," Swede said ominously, speaking clearly to me though his eyes never left the clerk, "this 'smart guy' worships his God from a prison cell." Wisely, the two clerks fled the room.

Swede shifted his eyes to me. "And another thing. Quit using that adding machine to do sixth grade arithmetic. Bring that book here."

Quickly, I handed him the text. He motioned me to a chair near his desk. For the rest of that evening, I listened with fascination while he talked of the magic of mathematics. He had me call out groups of large numbers and enter them into the adding machine. Following only in his head, he could give me the correct sum at any point.

One of my problems required the product of 65 x 65. Swede glanced at it for a fraction of a second and said, "Four thousand two hundred twenty-five."

"How did you do that?" I exclaimed.

"Any number times itself is a 'square,'" he said. "There are tricks to squaring. Take the square of any two-digit number ending in five. The last two numerals in the answer will always be twenty-five. So, in the number you're squaring, ignore the second digit, the fives, and concentrate on the first digit." He wrote down 65 x 65. Pointing with his pencil so I could follow each step, he continued. "Now, the first digit is six. Mentally add one to the first six making it seven, and then multiply that times the other six. What's the result?"

"Forty-two," I said.

"Right. And those are the first numerals in your answer. Since you know the last two numerals are twenty-five, your complete answer is four-two-two-five."

"You mean," I said with excitement, "that you always just add one to one of the first digits then multiply like you said?"

"Always."

Quickly, working in my head, I correctly squared numbers Swede called out. Later that evening, he explained other shortcuts for squaring even larger numbers, and, using what he called "the powers of ten," ways to mentally reduce large numbers to smaller ones for ease in multiplication and division. For the first time I sensed the excitement of mathematics.

Gradually, in the days that followed, I began taking difficult assignments to Swede. One evening at home, my father came to my room. Gently, but probingly, he questioned me at length about Swede. I told him about my homework and showed him a paper I had done in school that day—my first "A" in arithmetic. He studied the paper a moment, then smiled and left the room without further questions.

Years later, I learned what prompted my father's questions that evening. The deputy who had warned him earlier about Swede was concerned that I might be "idolizing a notorious gangster." The morning after talking to me, my father called the deputy to his office. "Porter," he said, "since Bill was born, I've been a sheriff, a United States Marshal, or warden of a maximum security penitentiary. He'll never have any 'idols' in a place like this. As for Garrison, I wouldn't be alive today if I couldn't trust my judgment of men. I know what he's doing . . . and why. Leave this to me."

And so, my sessions with Swede continued. Until I graduated from high school seven years later, that bleak prison office, with its barred windows and improbable teacher, became a classroom to me as real and as challenging as any I attended before or since.

One Friday evening as we worked, Swede was unduly solemn. Several times he appeared about to say something, then changed his mind. I happened to mention that my father and the entire family were going to Louisville the next day on business. At once, I sensed that for some reason Swede was relieved.

On the next afternoon, while we were away, three inmates attacked a guard and forced their way into the administration building, where they seized weapons. Thus armed, they attempted to shoot their way out of the institution. They reached the front steps, where two of them were shot and killed by guards and the third surrendered.

Later that day, when we returned home and learned what had happened, I recalled Swede's strange behavior the day before. Dutifully, I told my father. Swede was interrogated at once. Although he admitted he had heard rumors of a planned breakout, he was cleared of any collusion. His preoccupation was caused by fear that I might be in the administration building when the break occurred.

As I progressed through high school, our studies broadened. A voracious reader, Swede was ever recommending books and reminding me what bridges they could be. "They're my escape," he would say and grin at the irony.

Unlike many convicts, Swede made no claim of innocence. Once, while discussing my sociology assignment, I asked him if he agreed that poverty was the root of crime.

"No," he replied emphatically. "It's greed." We explored his contention that men willing to work hard for fair wages seldom see the inside of prisons. To test his theory, we researched hundreds of inmate files, tabulating the backgrounds of convicted men against their contemporaries who had never run afoul of the law but who had sprung from the same environment. Years later, the results of that research provided me with a controversial, but respected, college paper.

Swede delighted in engaging me in debate. One evening, he asked me if I approved of capital punishment.

"Yes," I replied.

"Does it stop violent crime?"

"It sure stops violent criminals." I voiced a cliché of the hardliners.

"Doesn't a locked cell do the same?"

"But what about the victims?" I countered. "Don't they deserve justice?"

"Justice? Or revenge? Does either justify further killing?"

"Swede," I began firmly, "the state has the right . . ."

He lifted a hand, stopping me in mid-sentence. "State is a euphemism, Bill. Legally or illegally, men execute men . . ." he gazed out of the barred window, ". . . and bear the consequences."

It was a conversation I was destined to recall many times years later, during the final decade of my father's life. In his 17-year tenure as warden, my father supervised 51 legal executions. He came to abhor capital punishment and was distressed by the dehumanizing anguish often suffered by those who, in the name of the "state," had to carry out the sentence. In his later years as warden, and after his retirement in 1956, his views were sought by many legislative and judicial leaders, including a fellow-Kentuckian, United States Chief Justice Fred Vincent, and Vincent's successor, Earl Warren.

My father didn't live to see his views prevail. But at his death in 1962, the Kentucky legislature cited his long crusade for penal reform, adjourned for the day in his memory, unanimously expressing by special resolution that Jesse Buchanan was "truly his brother's keeper." What no one else knew at the time was that some of the arguments my father used came, through me, from a convicted murderer with whom I had debated the issues years earlier.

As World War II engulfed the early 1940s, Swede and I taped up a world map and charted opposing forces. No major campaign escaped Swede's scrutiny. When Rommel swept boldly across North Africa, Swede paid the German field marshal a high compliment: "What a rumrunner he would have made!"

My graduation approached, and with it the certainty that I would soon leave for military service. Swede subtly switched the emphasis of our talks. Academics gave way to advice. The do's and don'ts took on a sharper ring of truth, coming from one who had violated most of the don'ts.

Soon after my 18th birthday, I received a set of silver lapel wings, token of my acceptance as an Army aviation cadet. Proudly, I showed them to Swede. He held the small cardboard box in his hand, quietly studying the ornament. In a moment he said, "What a small package to have such a big price tag!" Then, looking at me seriously, he said, "Life unfolds for most of us in a clear choice of packages, Bill, each with its own price tag. If you're tempted to grab one that glitters a bit too much, remember me and the others in here who ignored the price tags."

In March 1944, I received my call to the Air Corps. The day before I was to leave, my father called me to his office. He handed me Swede's file. I'd seen it many times, but now there was an added attachment, a description of the person who had perished in the casino firebombing years before.

"Swede didn't want you to see it," my father said. "But I think you should."

I studied the attachment silently. The victim had been a five-year old child.

"Swede came to me years ago," my father said. "He asked permission to help you with your schoolwork. He felt that by doing that he might in some way atone for the other youngster's death." He paused. "I'd say that, as far as it's possible, he's gone a long way toward doing just that."

I could only nod in agreement.

That evening, exactly seven years from the day I first saw him, I went to say goodbye to Swede. Then, I held out my hand. He grasped it firmly in both his. Standing there, taller than Swede now, I suddenly realized how much he had changed. The granite face bore deep markings of time passed in incarceration. The still close-cropped hair was thinner and gray.

After a moment, Swede smiled. Then, without a word, he released my hand and walked away down the long corridor toward his cellblock. I never saw him again. But I did hear from him once more, under strange circumstances, years later.

In 1952, Swede was transferred on an old charge to another state and imprisoned anew. Assigned to a menial job in the prison garage, he promptly escaped. Within hours he was listed throughout the country on the FBI's

Ten Most Wanted list and described as "dangerous as a rattlesnake."

A few months later, my hometown paper reported my completion of advanced degree studies and embarkation upon a regular Air Force career. One evening, in my apartment where I was stationed in St. Albans, Vermont, my phone rang. When I answered, a familiar voice from the past said without introduction, "I've been reading about you, Lieutenant."

"Swede! Where are you?"

He laughed. "Let's just say I'm calling long distance."

Hurriedly, we talked of many things, especially my father. "He's a great man, Bill. Tell him I said that." Then, finally, he asked, "By the way, do you still have that little package with your cadet wings?"

"It's around somewhere," I said.

"Well, from what I read about you, you can mark it 'price paid in full.' So long, Bill." Click.

I called my father immediately. He listened as I related my talk with Swede. After a long silence he said, "As far as I'm concerned, Swede has 'paid in full' too."

That was the last I ever heard from my convict tutor. But I will never forget him or the immeasurable debt he tried to pay, through me.

Postscript: While writing this article, I learned from authorities that Swede was recaptured in 1953, served his time and was released in 1964. He became an accountant in a small town in Alabama, where he died in 1969, a respected member of the community.

"Wisdom is not wisdom when it is derived from books alone."

—*Horace*

State of Mind

Laura Mehl

Although my hands are cuffed
and my feet are shackled,
this prison is just a "state of mind."
The wall in front of me
is just a wall,
nothing more at all.
Surrounded by barbed-wire fence,
I choose to see the beauty on both sides.

For I have come to appreciate
the warmth of a smile
and the heartache of a tear.
For we are all equal
and only divided
when love is not present.

Any prison is just a "state of mind,"
to me—I will never
let anyone cuff and shackle my soul,
and so I am
forever free.

*"Thoughts have power; thoughts are energy. And
you can make your world or break it by your own
thinking."*

—*Susan Taylor*

The Best Possible Gift

Douglas Burgess

The sight of only one impoverished child can make people want to give all they have to prevent another child from going without clean clothes, a hot meal, or toys to play with. I felt this way every time I saw a commercial asking for money to support a needy child in some distant land. I always regretted the fact that I couldn't help.

You see, I'm a prisoner. And despite what you may have heard, not every prisoner is an unfeeling, bloodthirsty monster—at least, not most of the men at the Kinross Correctional Facility in Michigan's isolated North Country.

Here at this prison, the Child of the Month Club was born. Since the club was created to help some of the area's neediest children and its mission echoed my own beliefs, I gladly joined in collecting soft-drink bottles, selling hamburgers, and sponsoring six-mile races to earn money for our kids.

Twice a year, the warden allowed us to bring 50 of the neediest children, parents, and guardians into the prison. Every September, we fed them thick slices of pizza and huge bowls of ice cream. Then we'd give the parents gift certificates for the discounted purchase of school supplies and clothing. But the breaking open of a large piñata was always the evening's highlight. Watching the children scoop up armfuls of the thousands of brightly colored candies would boost my spirits for months.

The most emotional and fulfilling event was saved for Christmas. Every Christmas we served our hungry charges heaping mounds of turkey and dressing and pie with ice cream. Any leftovers were put into containers for them to take home. Then, as the plates were being cleared from the tables, someone would begin to sing, "Here Comes Santa Claus," and one of our portly members would come bouncing into the room dressed as the jolly old elf, asking for all the good little boys and girls to follow him.

The eager kids always raced after him as he mounted his chair and began passing out bags filled with cookies and candy. Then Santa would point the children in our direction where we had hidden hundreds of packaged toys. The wide-eyed look that lit up every face when they saw the piles of colorfully wrapped boxes always melted my heart.

Not all of the giving was one-sided though. I remember one party where a mother brought in her newborn child. During the evening, she gently placed her tiny baby into the arms of a club member who hadn't held such a precious gift since the birth of his own baby twenty years earlier.

As he gazed down at that miracle entrusted to his care, he began to cry. Great tears of joy ran down his cheeks and disappeared into his graying beard. Those of us standing around were also moved to tears as we beheld what we had given up by coming to prison.

"Children are love made visible."
—*American Proverb*

THE IN SIDE
by Matt Matteo

Reprinted by permission of Matt Matteo.

"In every child who is born, no matter what circumstances, and no matter what parents, the potentiality of the human race is born again."

—James Agee

Santa's Unlikely Helpers

Douglas Burgess

An article appeared in The Saginaw News, requesting clothing for dozens of families who had lost everything in a recent flood. These unfortunate, displaced people were reduced to living in evacuation shelters. Only the most insensitive beast would not respond generously to such a plea for help.

At the Saginaw prison, three of us decided to find some way to provide assistance to these victims. But the challenges of trying to gain the prison administration's approval seemed insurmountable. Even worse, we wondered how our idea would be received by hundreds of alleged hardened criminals. Despite these worries, we began to plan.

After one quick meeting, we convinced the administration that we weren't trying to pull something mischievous, and they gave us the green light to proceed with our clothing drive. Convincing our peers to part with what little they had was, by far, our most difficult task.

To publicize our upcoming event, we posted flyers all over the compound. To our disappointment, most of the inmates remained oblivious. In an act born of desperation, we chose to announce our presence in a flamboyant way that no one could ignore—by becoming Santa's little elves.

We managed to get our hands on an old Santa suit, several bags of fabric scraps, and plenty of wrapping paper. With these odds and ends and a rickety sewing machine, we created elfin outfits, complete with pointy hats for our two convicts-turned-Santas. Finally out of two extra cartons, we made a huge donation box that resembled a wrapped gift.

On the day of our event, we had snow well up to our knees. We donned our outfits and stood on the sidewalk outside, begging for donations. As fellow inmates walked by, they started getting into the act. Soon cries of, "Ho, Ho, Ho!" rang out across the prison.

One of our teachers gave us a bell to ring. Someone else brought out a cassette player with Christmas songs set to a rap-beat. Soon we had an entire cast of impromptu dancers and more donations than our bags could hold.

By day's end, besides turning blue from the cold, we counted nearly a thousand useable items that we could donate to the flood victims. As we bagged the shirts and shoes, pants and hats, we commented on the success of our project. Those who scoffed at the notion of giving to a stranger eventually turned up to give something.

The highlight came when one man said to his friend, "It's the right thing to do. When I was between jobs and penniless, I lived in a shelter. The Salvation Army gave me this coat. Now I'm returning the favor." His friend left. Ten minutes later, he came back to donate his own bag of clothes.

[EDITOR'S NOTE: For information about The Salvation Army, contact your local phone directory or see Web site: http://www.salvationarmy.org/.]

"Give what you have to somebody; it may be better than you think."
—*Henry Wadsworth Longfellow*

Three Shanks

Troy Evans

W hile serving seven and a half years in federal prison for armed bank robbery, I was faced with constant threats, challenges, and tough decisions. The inmates had almost total run of the institution. I'm a big guy. I like to think I can take care of myself, but I'm not too proud to tell you that I spent hours hunkered behind a four-foot-tall locker in my prison cell.

Every time that cell door was flung open, I prayed nobody would come any farther. People were often dragged out of their cells, beaten, stabbed and killed for no reason. So, when three gang members rolled in on me and uttered, "It's time to make a decision, or else!" I assure you, they meant business.

Each was carrying a shank—something used to kill one another in prison. The first guy was carrying a toothbrush, filed to a very sharp point, the second had a razor-sharp pork chop bone, and the third one carried a 16-penny nail driven through a six-inch piece of broom handle.

As they entered my cell I trembled in terror. My gut reaction was to do anything they asked. I wanted to live. But then something much stronger than fear came over me.

I saw the face of my son and remembered how committed he was to me, regardless of where I was. I thought about my mom and my dad, and the promise I made to them to turn my life around. I knew how much my family had sacrificed for me in the past. How I ached to be the person that my son saw me to be—the person my parents rediscovered in me! Somehow these feelings washed away the terror.

Suddenly the sound of jingling keys echoed down the corridor. The trio quickly shoved their shanks under my mattress. Since only two inmates were allowed in a cell at any one time, the correctional officer stuck his head in and barked, "Evans . . . what are these guys doing in your cell?"

"They're not doing anything, sir. We're just kickin' it," I answered, trying to act natural. "They're not doing anything at all."

"Out of Evan's cell," he shouted.

Five minutes later, when the coast was clear, I gathered up the three shanks, and one at a time, returned them back to their rightful owners, adding, "I think you forgot something."

They never bothered me again. I don't know why. Maybe because I didn't tell the correctional officer what they were doing in my cell—or perhaps they saw in my eyes that I wasn't going to take that easy road again. They would have to finish the job they set out to do. Whatever their reasons, I was grateful.

Those three gang members who rolled in on me— who came to take my life if I weren't willing to sling their drugs—came to me several years later. They pleaded with me to help them to accomplish what I was achieving. They wanted me to help them attain scholarships so they too could seek an education.

THE IN SIDE
by Matt Matteo

Reprinted by permission of Matt Matteo.

"Cherish your visions and your dreams, as they are the children of your soul, the blue-prints of your ultimate achievements."

—Napoleon Hill

About Tom Lagana

Tom Lagana believes that one person can make a difference. He is dedicated to living a positive, successful life and helping others to do the same.

He has volunteered extensively in the prison system throughout the United States, working with inmates. He is also a narrator for the Delaware Division for the Visually Impaired, and is a volunteer in the Emergency Department of Christiana Care's Hospital, in Wilmington, Delaware. In 1994, he was honored as a recipient of the Jefferson Award for outstanding public service.

Tom graduated from Villanova University in Pennsylvania with a degree in electrical engineering and worked as an engineer for more than 30 years. In 1997, he attended Jack Canfield's Facilitation Skills Seminar and returned in 1998 to serve as an assistant.

Since then, he has facilitated more than 1,000 personal development and management presentations nationally and internationally. Through his refreshingly humorous presentations, laced with innovative audience interactions, Tom inspires people everywhere to become even better than their best.

Tom's life experiences have led him to co-author two highly successful books in the best-selling *Chicken Soup for the Soul* Series: *Chicken Soup for the Volunteer's Soul* and *Chicken Soup for the Prisoner's Soul.*

Tom Lagana
P.O. Box 7816
Wilmington, DE 19803
302-475-4825
E-mail: Tom@TomLagana.com
Web site: http://www.TomLagana.com

About Laura Lagana

*L*aura Lagana, a professional speaker, registered nurse and volunteer, is author and editor of *Touched by Angels of Mercy,* co-author of *Chicken Soup for the Volunteer's Soul,* and a frequent contributor to the best-selling *Chicken Soup for the Soul* series.

Connecting to her audiences with a warm heart and encouraging message, Laura brings energy and enthusiasm to her audience as she shares personal stories and information on topics ranging from stress mastery to making a difference in our world.

As a humanitarian, she has learned first-hand about the far-reaching, positive effects of beneficence—from providing a newfound sense of purpose to honoring the dignity and tenacity of the terminally ill and the elderly.

After working for 28 years as a registered nurse, oftentimes aided by valiant volunteers, and 40 years as a volunteer, Laura admits to receiving far more than she has given. Through the years, she has gained sharp insight into the human condition, along with new opportunities to make a positive difference.

Ecstatic about combining her nursing expertise with a passion for writing and speaking, Laura applies the skill and knowledge gleaned from her lifelong journey of unique, life-changing experiences to help others become their best.

Laura Lagana
P.O. Box 7816
Wilmington, DE 19803
302-475-4825
E-mail: Laura@LauraLagana.com
Web site: http://www.LauraLagana.com

Programs & Resources

In addition to the programs and resources mentioned below appropriate stories, the following are also recommended:

Prisoner's Soul Programs: Interactive presentation for inmates, prison staff and volunteers to improve goal setting, effective communication and conflict resolution skills to promote peak performance and peaceful environments. Contact: Tom Lagana, co-author, *Chicken Soup for the Prisoner's Soul*, P.O. Box 7816, Wilmington, DE 19803, e-mail: Tom@TomLagana.com, Web site: http://www.TomLagana.com

Thresholds: A six-step decision-making course in prison. Contact: Thresholds in Delaware County, P.O. Box 334, Media, PA 19063, Web site: http://www.thresholdsdelco.org

Taking Flight: Helps people organize and form Toastmasters clubs in prisons. Contact: Paul Jagen, 409-886-6769, e-mail: pjagen@gt.rr.com

Brian Brookheart Ministries: Brian Brookheart, author of *A Prisoner: Released,* PMB #509, 44 Music Square East, Nashville, TN 37203

Children of Prisoners Library (CPL): The Family & Corrections Network (FCN) has the library available on-line. CPL provides 19 free information sheets designed for people serving children of prisoners and their caregivers. Information sheets may be downloaded, duplicated and distributed without charge, but may not be altered or sold. FCN is not budgeted to mail free copies. Go to http://www.fcnetwork.org and click Libraries, then select, Children of Prisoners Library. Contact: Family and Corrections Network, 32 Oak Grove Road, Palmyra, VA 22963, e-mail: fcn@fcnetwork.org, Web site: http://www.fcnetwork.org

Correspondence Programs for Inmates: Reference book: *Prisoners' Guerrilla Handbook to Correspondence Programs in the United States and Canada* by Jon Marc Taylor. Contact: Biddle Publishing Company, 13 Gurnet Road, PMB 103, Brunswick, ME 04011, Web site: http://www.biddle-audenreed.com

"10 Ways to be a Better Dad" and "Creating a Father-Friendly Neighborhood: 10 Things You Can Do" brochures. Contact: National Fatherhood Initiative, 101 Lake Forest Boulevard, Suite 360, Gaithersburg, MD 20877, Web site: http://www.fatherhood.org

Stages of The Total Truth Process

1. Anger and Resentment (tantrum)
I'm angry that . . .   I'm fed up with . . .
I hate it when . . .   I resent . . .
I don't like it when . . .   I can't stand . . .

2. Hurt
It hurt me when . . .   I feel awful about . . .
I feel hurt that . . .   I felt sad when . . .
I feel sad when . . .   I feel disappointed about . . .

3. Fear
I was afraid that . . .   I'm afraid that . . .
I feel scared when . . .   I get afraid of you when . . .

4. Remorse, Regret, Accountability
I'm sorry that . . .   I'm sorry for . . .
Please forgive me for . . .   I didn't mean to . . .

5. Wants
All I ever want(ed) . . .   I want(ed) . . .
I want you to . . .   I deserve . . .

6. Love, Compassion, Forgiveness and Appreciation
I understand that . . .   I forgive you for . . .
I appreciate . . .   Thank you for . . .
I love you because . . .   I love you when . . .
I forgive you for . . . and I forgive myself for . . .

Reprinted by permission of Jack Canfield. ©1997 Jack Canfield.

Contributing Authors & Cartoonists

Joan Wester Anderson is a magazine writer and author of 14 books. *Where Angels Walk,* was on the *New York Times* best-seller list for more than a year. She runs an angel Web site, http://www.joanwanderson.com, which sends a new story each week to her subscriber list. Contact her at e-mail: joan@joanwanderson.com.

Eric F. Bauman is a social worker and alcohol counselor at the Nassau County Sheriff's Office. He has five children and is expecting his sixth. His wife, Palma, is truly the hero of his family. He is director of the Sheriff's Employee Assistance Program. He now works primarily with correctional staff and their families who are experiencing personal problems. He is a correctional officer and lives on Long Island, New York.

Kim Book is a prison volunteer in Delaware for Prison Fellowship Ministries and Correctional Facility Pre-Release and Victim Sensitivity Programs. She has been a trained mediator for five years and is working on a mediation program that will bring together victims and offenders of violent crimes. Contact her at 220 Beiser Blvd., Dover, DE 19904; e-mail: JOCKOKIM@aol.com.

Roy Anthony Borges is a 1998 First-Place Amy Award Winner and author of *Faith and Love Behind Prison Fences.* He may be contacted at elainenewbold@aol.com or #029381 Washington Correctional Institute, 4455 Sam Mitchell Drive, Chipley, FL 32428.

Michael Bowler has two master's degrees (film/television and special education). He is a high school special education teacher. A Big Brother with Catholic Big Brothers Big Sisters for 20 years, he has mentored seven boys. He has been a youth detention volunteer for 19 years at juvenile halls, camps, placements, prisons, and the youth authority. Contact him at 16350 Filbert Street, Sylmar, CA 91342.

William J. Buchanan is the author of *Execution Eve* and five other books, three of which have been made into movies. His father was a warden for 20 years. Bill lives in Albuquerque, New Mexico. Contact him by e-mail at kagy12@comcast.net or Web site: http://www.buchanan.scriptmania.com.

Douglas Burgess is serving a life sentence for a crime he committed while on leave from the Marine Corps in 1984. He is committed to atoning for his past misdeeds through programs benefiting homeless shelters, food banks, and youthful offenders. He is currently earning a master's degree and writing his second book. Contact him at #178559 KCF, 16770 S. Watertower, Kincheloe, MI 49788.

Burl Cain, CCE, is Warden of Louisiana State Penitentiary. He is a Certified Corrections Executive and a graduate of Louisiana State University. Warden Cain is nationally recognized as being one of the most innovative professionals in his field and was named to Louisiana's Political Hall of Fame and Warden of the Year in 2003. He is married and the father of three. Contact him at Louisiana State Penitentiary, Angola, LA 70712.

Jack Canfield is the founder and co-creator of the *New York Times* #1 best-selling *Chicken Soup for the Soul*® book series. He is also the founder of Self-Esteem Seminars, located in Santa Barbara, California, which train entrepreneurs, educators, corporate leaders and employees how to accelerate the achievement of their personal and professional goals. See Web sites: http://www.chickensoup.com and http://www.jackcanfield.com.

Antoinette (Toni) Carter is a PRE-GED teacher in the Education Program at Folsom State Prison in Represa, California. In 1992, she received the Outstanding Academic Teacher of the Year Award. She may be contacted at P.O. Box 983, Roseville, CA 95678; e-mail: netnuts@quiknet.com.

Rev. Rod Carter is the director of the Restorative Justice Program at Queen's Theological College. He was formerly regional chaplain for the Correctional Service of Canada for five years. An ex-offender, he received a criminal Pardon in 1977. He is a contributing author in *Chicken Soup for the Prisoner's Soul.* Contact him at Queen's Theological College, 1000 University Ave., Kingston, Ontario K7L 3N6, Canada; e-mail: carterr@post.queensu.ca.

Danny Edward Scott Casalenuovo is serving a five-year term. He is a member of the Tutoring Counsel Committee, teaching language and math to fellow inmates. He is employed in the prison's T-shirt factory and working on building his life from the inside out. Contact him at T-11006, California Men's Colony State Prison, P.O. Box 8101 #6238, San Luis Obispo, CA 93409-8101.

George Castillo was a prison chaplain for more than 20 years. His book, *My Life Between The Cross And The Bars,* has inspirational stories of life-changing experiences, which led him to advocate prison reform. Contact him at G & M Publications, P.O. Box 657, Shalimar, FL 32579; his Web site: http://www.castilloBook.com; or by e-mail: g-mpub@cox.net.

Marcus Cater is a single father of two daughters and a disabled veteran of the army. He served five years in prison and is looking forward to being a positive member of society once again. He can be contacted at P.O. Box 934, Prineville, OR 97754.

Mike Chernock is a management consultant during the week but every other Sunday since 1995 has teamed up with friends to conduct church services and baptisms and share Eucharist at the San Quentin hospital and HIV ward. He can be reached via his Web site: http://www.uscconsulting.com or by e-mail: Michael@ChernockAssociates.com.

Charles Colson was a well known public figure, convicted and imprisoned for seven months because of his involvement in the Watergate scandal as Nixon's Special Counsel. A year after his release he started a prison ministry. In 1993, he was awarded the Templeton Prize for Progress in Religion. He is now a nationally recognized speaker and founder of Prison Fellowship®. He may be contacted through his Web site: http://www.prisonfellowship.org.

Diane Cook is a speaker/dramatist and award-winning journalist. She is executive director of Word Warrior Ministries, Inc., an evangelical performing arts and speaking outreach. The amateur arm, CTM Players, performs in nursing homes, prisons, and churches. Diane lives in Dover, Delaware with her family. Contact her at P.O. Box 365, Cheswold, DE 19936; by e-mail: dcookwrites@cookworkshop.com; Web site: http://www.cookworkshop.com.

Shelly Currier is a registered nurse with 22 years of experience and now working at the Chaves County Detention Center. She is part of the Crossings Program, a faith-based ministry at the Roswell Correctional Center in New Mexico. She also tutors at-risk teens who are part of the Youth ChalleNGe Program run by the National Guard. Contact her at e-mail: Whippy@dfn.com.

Jane Davis is the founder and guide of HOPE-HOWSE International, Inc., a 501c3 non-profit organization, dedicated to creating peace through the integration of honesty, faith and action. Contact her at P.O. Box 9855; Santa Fe, NM 87504; e-mail: jane@hope-howse.org; or though her Web site at: http://www.hope-howse.org.

Troy Evans is a professional speaker, author and ex-inmate. He is author of *From Desperation to Dedication: Lessons You Can Bank On*. He may be contacted at The Evans Group, 3104 E. Camelback Road #436, Phoenix, AZ 85016, e-mail: troy@troyevans.com; Web site: http://www.troyevans.com.

Gary K. Farlow is a native Tarheel with a juris doctorate from Heed University. His works have appeared in two *Chicken Soup for the Soul* books and two poetic anthologies. He is author of *Prison-ese: A Survivor's Guide to Speaking Slang*. His works, *Conferring With The Moon* and *After Midnight*, two volumes of poetry, may be ordered from Carolyn Jackson, 915 Benjamin Benson St., Greensboro, NC 27406.

Cathy Fontenot, CCE, is an Assistant Warden of Programming at the Louisiana State Penitentiary. She has worked in corrections for eleven years and holds a Bachelor's Degree in Criminal Justice from the University of Southwestern Louisiana. She is a Certified Corrections Executive and serves as a prison auditor for the American Correctional Association. She is married and the mother to two small children. She may be contacted through e-mail at: cathyfontenot@oyd01.corrections.state.la.us.

Jerry Gillies, a former journalist (NBC-New York), is the author of six books on personal development and relationships, including the best-selling *Moneylove* (Warner Books). For over twenty years, he conducted seminars and gave lectures across the U.S., Canada, England, and South Africa. He may be contacted at Jerry Gillies K46460, Folsom State Prison, Bldg. 5/AB1-01, P.O. Box 715071, Represa, CA 95671-5071.

Debby Giusti is a medical technologist and freelance writer who lives in the Atlanta area. Her work has appeared in numerous publications, including *Advance Magazine for Administrators of the Laboratory, Southern Lady, Woman's World, Army Magazine, Family, Our Sunday Visitor,* and *Chicken Soup for the Volunteer's Soul.*

Soren Gordhamer founded the Lineage Project, a south Bronx non-profit organization that teaches awareness practices to at-risk and incarcerated teens (www.lineageproject.org). He is author of the meditation book for teens, *Just Say OM!* (Adams Media, 2001). Contact him at e-mail: soren@lineageproject.org or The Lineage Project, 509 Willis Avenue, Bronx, NY 10455; e-mail: info@lineageproject.org.

Shannon Grillo has more than 60 certificates in self-help and vocational areas. She has an Associate of General Studies degree and made the National Dean's List. She is a "class project" for a high school class in Layton, Utah, and teaches them that life is about choice. Contact her at Shannon Grillo #40805, 4370 Smiley Road, Las Vegas, NV 89115.

Jean Hull Herman is editor of *Mobius, The Poetry Magazine.* In 2002, her first book, *Starving for the Marvelous,* won first prize in the National Federation of Press Women competition for poetry. She may be contacted at P. O. 7544, Wilmington, DE 19803; Web site: www.MobiusPoetry.com.

Thomas Ann Hines is a certified criminal justice specialist. She has received numerous awards, including the highest volunteer award given by the then Governor George W. Bush. She has spoken in prisons and juvenile facilities since 1994, and has been a guest on the Oprah Winfrey show. Contact her at P.O. Box 864499, Plano, TX 75086-4499; e-mail: TAHines@aol.com.

Steve C. Hokonson is a graduate of Washington State University (Wazzu) and Pacific Lutheran Theological Seminary. He loves grandkids, tennis, music, reading, and yard work. He is blessed with a loving, extremely creative spouse, Nancy, who makes life a joy. He finds chaplaincy and corrections the perfect fit for finding gifts and challenges in everyday life. Contact him by e-mail at: shokonso@ll.doc.state.mn.us.

Joan K. Johnson is a retired administrative assistant from the University of California and San Diego State University. She lives in Sedona, Arizona, and has two other children, Mike and Kimberly, and five grandchildren. She may be contacted by e-mail: alohajoanj@aol.com.

Jane Katenkamp and her husband, Jack, have been married for over 40 years, and they have five children and ten grandchildren. They have led over 185 programs in prison. Since 1981 they have been the coordinating couple for National Marriage Encounter Prison Ministry. Jane is author of *Respecting Life: An Activity Guide.* Contact her at P.O. Box 53583, Cincinnati, OH 45253; e-mail: jane.jack7@juno.com.

Pooja Krishna is a banker, who writes in her spare time. She has been involved in a variety of community support initiatives including those for the visually impaired and Adult Literacy. She may be contacted at e-mail: pooja_nvk@hotmail.com.

Laura Lagana is a professional speaker, author, registered nurse and volunteer. She is co-author of *Chicken Soup for the Volunteer's Soul,* author/ editor of *Touched by Angels of Mercy,* and a frequent contributor to the best-selling *Chicken Soup for the Soul* series. Contact her at P.O. Box 7816, Wilmington, DE 19803; e-mail: Laura@LauraLagana.com; or her Web site: http://www.LauraLagana.com.

Tom Lagana is a professional speaker, author and engineer. He has been a prison volunteer for more than ten years. He is co-author of *Chicken Soup for the Prisoner's Soul* and *Chicken Soup for the Volunteer's Soul.* Contact him at e-mail: Tom@TomLagana.com; Web site: www.TomLagana.com; or P.O. Box 7816, Wilmington, DE 19803.

Linda Larsen is a highly sought-after speaker and trainer specializing in communication, conflict management, motivation, and self-esteem. She is the author of an audio program, *12 Secrets to High Self-Esteem,* and the book, *True Power.* Contact her at e-mail: lindalarsen@lindalarsen.com; Web site: http://www.lindalarsen.com.

Kay Lee is a late-blooming grandmother on a personal "Journey for Justice." She may be contacted through Making The Walls Transparent, e-mail: kaylee1@charter.net; Web site: http://www.angelfire.com/fl3/starke.

Dave LeFave is an inmate in the Colorado Department of Corrections. He has written numerous poems and prides himself on staying positive and trying to make the most of any situation. He may be contacted at #86651, P.O. Box 6000, Sterling, CO 80751.

Mary V. Leftridge Byrd has served in criminal justice agencies and departments for more than 25 years. She is a former warden and currently serves as Deputy Secretary with the Pennsylvania Department of Corrections. She may be contacted at e-mail: mleftridge@state.pa.us.

Mary G. Lodge is a mother to five children, eleven grandchildren, and four great-children. She enjoys crafts, painting and writing. She is a Stephan Minister in her church and enjoys speaking on the subject of forgiveness. She may be contacted at e-mail: LodgeDoor@aol.com.

Matt Matteo is an award-winning artist, author of two cartoon series, book illustrator, and adult tutor from Derry, Pennsylvania. He is a contributing artist in *Chicken Soup for the Prisoner's Soul*, *Chicken Soup for the Volunteer's Soul*, and *Touched by Angels of Mercy*. He contributes much of his work to benefit charities. Contact him at 801 Butler Pike – BS-7345, Mercer, PA 16137.

Ray McKeon is the Director of Detention Ministry for the Archdiocese of San Francisco office of Public Policy/Social Concerns/Detention Ministry. He may be contacted at One Peter Yorke Way, San Francisco, CA 94109-6602, 415-614-5569; Fax: 415-614-5568; e-mail: ray_mckeon@hotmail.com.

Laura Mehl relies on God and appreciates the support of her family and friends. She is a mother to three sons and is currently awaiting parole. She works as a drug/alcohol peer assistant at SCI-Cambridge Springs, while continuing to be an aspiring artist and writer. Contact her at 200 Point Comfort Ave., Hampton, VA 23664.

Diane Hamill Metzger is a Pennsylvania life-sentenced prisoner in her 28th year of incarceration. She has earned four college degrees, two apprenticeships and numerous educational, literary, and community service awards. She is a published writer, poet and lyricist, a member of MENSA and ASCAP and the mother of a grown son. Contact her at 660 Baylor Blvd., New Castle, DE 19720.

Sandra Milholland, M.S., M.MFT., is an associate clinical psychologist for the Texas Department of Criminal Justice. She is a licensed marriage and family therapist, licensed professional counselor, and free-lance writer. She and her husband, Tom, co-authored *Prelude to Joy: Making Your Marriage A Heavenly One* (Covenant Publishing, 2002).

Contributing Authors & Cartoonists (cont.)

Dan Millstein is the founding director of Visions for Prisons, a non-profit 501(3)c organization and founder of the Peace in Prison project. He is a speaker and seminar leader, writer, visionary, and consultant to businesses and individuals both in the Americas and Europe. Contact him at P.O. Box 1631, Costa Mesa, CA 92628; by e-mail at: vfp95@aol.com; or his Web site: http://www.visionsforprisons.org.

Ken "Duke" Monse'Broten, pen name Edwin Allen Lee, is a grandfather and great grandfather originally from Park River, North Dakota. He has written numerous articles and short stories. Ken is author of *Messages from the Heart*, co-author of *Cissy's Magic*, and contributing author in *Chicken Soup for the Prisoner's Soul* and *Touched by Angels of Mercy*. Contact him at #3571494, Snake River Correctional Institute, 777 Stanton Blvd. Ontario, OR 97914.

Tom Prisk has been a published cartoonist since 1977. His work has appeared in the *Saturday Evening Post, The Best Cartoons from the Saturday Evening Post, Woman's World, Reader's Digest, Yankee Magazine, Writer's Digest, Leadership* and the *Best Cartoons from Leadership,* among others. He is the assistant chaplain at Marquette Branch Prison. Contact him at e-mail: tprisk@up.net.

Mary Rachelski and her husband, Andy, have been involved in prison ministry since 1989. She volunteered for nine years, several days a week, in the Institute Activities Coordinator's office before recently accepting that position. Contact her at Missouri Eastern Correctional Center, 18701 Old Highway 66, Pacific, MO 63069; e-mail: jailbirdlady@att.com.

Marcia Reynolds, M.A., M.Ed., author of *How to Outsmart Your Brain,* provides workshops, presentations and coaching designed to help people forge strong relationships, increase their financial rewards, and feel the pleasure of success in their lives. You can read more about her books and services at Web site: http://www.OutsmartYourBrain.com.

Cathy Roberts, CCM, is Administrative Manager of the Mail/Package Department at the Louisiana State Penitentiary. She has been employed with Corrections for 27 years and is a Certified Corrections Manager. She is married and the mother of three. She is the editor of the *B Line News,* which circulates to the employee residents of Angola. Contact her at Louisiana State Penitentiary Mail/Package Dept., Angola, LA 70712.

David Roth's resume´ includes 8 Wind River CDs, a 1994 NAIRD "Indie" nomination (singer/songwriter Album of the Year), song lyrics in several *Chicken Soup for the Soul* books, and top honors at two of the country's premier songwriter competitions. He may be contacted at David Roth/Maythelight Music, P.O. Box 495, Orleans, MA 02653, e-mail: RothDM@aol.com; Web site: http://www.davidrothmusic.com.

George M. Roth is a writer and inspiring motivational speaker. He presents dynamic seminars and keynote speeches which emphasize the value of acquiring new perspectives. He is a member of the Screen Actors Guild, the American Federation of Television and Radio Artists, and the National Speakers Association. Contact him at e-mail: gmr@georgeroth.com; Web site: http://www.georgeroth.com.

William Ryan is a 40-year-old inmate at the Newton Correctional Facility in Iowa. He tries his best to take care of his family, help others, and be a good citizen. He may be contacted at #803922, NCF Box 218, Newton, IA 50208.

Christian Snyder is currently serving a 5 to 15 year sentence in New York State. He launched a career in freelance cartooning while incarcerated. He has been published in numerous magazines and trade journals. Cartooning has been a positive rehabilitative tool for him, and he plans to pursue freelance cartooning as a full-time career upon his release.

LeAnn Thieman motivates people to make a difference in the world by sharing life-lessons from the Vietnam Orphan Airlift. She has been featured in *Newsweek* magazine, FOX-TV News, PAX-TV and ten *Chicken Soup for the Soul* books. She is co-author of *Chicken Soup for the Nurse's Soul, Chicken Soup for the Christian Woman's Soul,* and *Chicken Soup for the Caregiver's Soul.* Web site: http://www.LeAnnThieman.com.

Terrell L. Thomas is an aspiring author who has written numerous short stories and articles. He's currently working on his first novel and actively seeking an agent. He is an accomplished speaker through Toastmasters and Speech Crafters. He is working on his degree through Ohio University. Contact him at #6998603, SRCI, 777 Stanton Blvd., Ontario, OR 97914.

George Toth was born in Connecticut and has been around the USA three times. He is single. Contact him at #J78888, California Men's Colony State Prison, P.O. Box 8101; San Luis Obispo, CA 93409-8101.

Teresa Tyson is an Alternatives to Violence Project (AVP) facilitator and trainer. She has facilitated AVP Workshops on four continents in schools, prisons and communities. She is a Victim Offender Dialogue Facilitator for Crimes of Severe Violence for the state of Ohio. She may be contacted at e-mail: teresatyson@hotmail.com.

Permissions

Front Matter

The Prayer. Reprinted by permission of Roy Anthony Borges. ©2002 Roy Anthony Borges. Excerpted from *Faith and Love Behind Prison Fences.*

From the Far Side of the Wall. Reprinted by permission of Rod Carter. ©2003 Rod Carter.

Chapter 1

Serving Moral Time. Reprinted by permission of Gary K. Farlow. ©2003 Gary K. Farlow.

A Life that Matters. Reprinted by permission of Douglas Burgess. ©2000 Douglas Burgess.

Reading History. Reprinted by permission of Pooja Krishna. ©2000 Pooja Krishna.

A Life-Long Enterprise. Reprinted by permission of Diane Hamill Metzger. ©2000 Diane Hamill Metzger.

Just Say Yes. Reprinted by permission of Dan Millstein. ©2001 Dan Millstein.

A Ten-Cent Pen. Reprinted by permission of Matt Matteo. ©2003 Matt Matteo.

The Spirit of Tuck. Reprinted by permission of Kay Lee. ©2003 Kay Lee.

Reaching Beyond the Walls. Reprinted by permission of George Castillo. ©2003 George Castillo. Based on excerpts from *My Life Between The Cross And The Bars,* G & M Publications. ©1996, G & M Publications, P.O. Box 657, Shalimar, FL 32579.

An Unexpected Favor. Reprinted by permission of William Ryan. ©2003 William Ryan.

The Blind Project. Reprinted by permission of Jerry Gillies. ©2003 Jerry Gillies.

Chapter 2

His Brother's Keeper. Reprinted by permission of Cathy Fontenot. ©2003 Cathy Fontenot.

Chapter 3

Chapter 4

Covering Kids' Backs. Reprinted by permission of Mary V. Leftridge Byrd. ©2002 Mary V. Leftridge Byrd.

Checking In. Reprinted by permission of Steve C. Hokonson. ©2003 Steve C. Hokonson.

Angel Tree. Reprinted by permission of Terrell L. Thomas. ©2000 Terrell L. Thomas.

Another Peanut Butter Sandwich. Reprinted by permission of Charles W. Colson. ©1997 Charles W. Colson. Excerpted from *Loving God,* by Chuck Colson, Zondervan, 5300 Patterson SE, Grand Rapids, MI 49530; June 2, 1997, pp. 133.

A Time of Pain: A Time of Love. Reprinted by permission of Ray McKeon. ©1999 Ray McKeon.

They Call Her Granny. Reprinted by permission of Shelly Currier. ©2003 Shelly Currier.

Kindness Comes in Small Packages. Reprinted by permission of Laura Lagana ©2003 Laura Lagana.

Abundance of Love. Reprinted by permission of Joan K. Johnson. ©2000 Joan K. Johnson.

Chapter 5

Ode to a Six-Digit Number. Reprinted by permission of Sandra Milholland. ©2003 Sandra Milholland.

Amazing Grace. Reprinted by permission of Ken "Duke" Monse'Broten. Copyright ©2003 Ken "Duke" Monse'Broten. Based on excerpts from *Messages from the Heart* by Edwin Allen Lee.

The First Four Pages. Reprinted by permission of Marcus Cater ©2000 Marcus Cater.

Legal Advice. Reprinted by permission of Dave LeFave. ©2003 Dave LeFave.

Yoga-Man. Reprinted by permission of Soren Gordhamer. ©2002 Soren Gordhamer.

A Sign from God. Reprinted by permission of Jane Katenkamp. Copyright ©2003 Jane Katenkamp.

Conversion on the Job. Reprinted by permission of Eric F. Bauman. ©1995 Eric F. Bauman. Previously published in *Commonweal* magazine September 8, 1995.